Negotiations

Negotiations

Principles and Techniques

Neal W. Beckmann

Lexington Books
D.C. Heath and Company
Lexington, Massachusetts
Toronto

Library of Congress Cataloging in Publication Data

Beckmann, Neal W

    Negotiations: principles and techniques.

    Includes index.
    1. Purchasing. 2. Selling. Negotiation. I. Title.
HF5437.B39   658.4   77-93
ISBN 0-669-01437-0

Second printing August 1977.

Published simultaneously in Canada

Printed in the United States of America

International Standard Book Number: 0-669-01437-0

Library of Congress Catalog Card Number: 77-93

To my wife Jackie,
with whom I am
still negotiating

Contents

List of Figures

List of Schedules

Foreword

Twenty-five years ago the buyer-seller relationship was viewed almost, if not entirely, as an empirical art. It was widely accepted that success in the negotiation process was largely a matter of personality and of inherited abilities that were bestowed upon few individuals and/or learned through years of exposure to daily technical practice. Moreover, most people assumed that negotiations referred to a price discussion.

The idea that negotiation is a sequential process requiring thoughtful preparation, presentation and continuous evaluation is of recent vintage. In recent years it has become increasingly apparent that organized knowledge is just as important in the negotiation process as in other fields of endeavor. In fact, the successful negotiator today is compelled to assimilate a vast array of data and information, beyond price, that will assist him/her in gaining a competitive advantage.

This book combines theory and practice relative to the negotiation process. It offers a succinct approach for both the teacher and practitioner for developing expertise in the too often forgotten "core" of buying-selling negotiation. Readers who have extensive practical experience will be receptive to the psychological presentation of human behavior. Moreover, the extensive presentation of day-to-day strategies and procedures should provide a basis for self-evaluation of one's efficacy.

The textual matter also provides an excellent opportunity for students of purchasing and personal selling to develop analytical skills within their respective field. The author vividly presents the prerequisites, behavorial as well as organizational, necessary to effectuate a successful transaction process. The material is presented in fourteen easy to read chapters. Moreover, the actual application of theory to every day situations brings realism to the study process.

In sum, this book is a timely and effective presentation of principles and practices for both learned and novice practitioners and students of the art of negotiation. It will serve both well as an instructional resource and a reference source. The test of time and use may give it the professional distinction of being the text against which others will be judged.

Guy R. Banville
St. Louis University

Preface

This book is written for people in business and private life who have to solve problems and to make decisions involving other people or businesses. In recent years, specialists have studied the *art of negotiating* most intensively, and have brought some startling new insights to the process. But in doing so, they have often left the ordinary executive behind by speaking two languages that are generally unintelligible to those not especially trained in the field. The first language is analytical, and the second is the jargon of the behavioral sciences. This book is based upon thorough review of the specialized works, and converts them into practical terminology. The book also draws on the observations and findings of successful executives who have tried to analyze closely what they do when they negotiate.

This book will help to improve negotiating ability:

1. By explaining how to negotiate in very specific form. Negotiation can be described as a "give and take" discussion producing a mutually beneficial relationship; the discussion occurs when there is a difference between a present condition and a desired condition (or objective). So by knowing where you are and by setting an objective, you have cleared the stage for negotiation.
2. By making it clear that to achieve an objective, somebody has to make a commitment to somebody else whose opinion is important, that somebody will change something to bring the actual condition closer to the objective. In negotiations, somebody has to choose among alternative solutions and moves. The negotiator cannot delay, leaving things undone.
3. By using some analytical tools that order the facts and goals into a model for negotiation. The alternatives to such tools are emotion and intuition; they are not entirely eliminated, but they can be controlled better if there is a system.
4. By explaining how to negotiate to achieve the best results—the heart of the negotiation. Much of the analytical study of negotiating centers on this problem, but the basic process is logical and not purely analytical. The negotiator who understands the basic logic of the process can use it even if he has no analytical training. This book explains the basic logic of the process, using some simple illustrations that apply to negotiating.
5. By transforming this process into action that makes things happen, and by applying the results to the actual problems the executive faces in his job.

The best way to use this book is to read through it completely. If you are a manager, or use analysis in your work, the analytical segments will seem simple. If you are less adept at analysis, you can read the text, and, if the analysis seems esoteric, simply read right past it and return later to study it in more depth. The last section of the book summarizes the negotiating tools that apply to life in the plant, office, or home.

The purpose of this book is to teach. The training director who uses this text to teach the *art of negotiating* in a company goal program, may sharpen the skills of the managers on those special problem-solving objectives that emerge once the regular objectives are under control. By studying the book on his own, a manager should be better able to define his problems and to make the decisions necessary to solve them. If you learn, you should change your behavior, be more effective, achieve more of your objectives, and make more things happen.

All persons, businesses, and situations shown in this book are entirely fictitious. Any resemblance to any person living or dead or to any existing or previously existing business is coincidental. The author's purpose is to illustrate certain principles and techniques.

Neal W. Beckmann

Acknowledgments

A multitude of people have contributed to the experiences that led me to write this book. Recognizing that I cannot acknowledge everyone, I limit my expressions of special thanks to those most involved.

My sincere thanks to the many members of the Purchasing Management Association of St. Louis, and to the National Association of Purchasing Management, for the experiences that contributed to the foundation of this book. In particular, Harold K. Kramer, C.P.M., purchasing consultant and past President of the Purchasing Management Association of St. Louis, has been most helpful.

My thanks, also, to Richard D. Gilbert, LL.B., Group Vice President, BBC Health Care Facilities, a Division of Bank Building and Equipment Corporation of America, to William A. Heyward, and to my wife Jackie for their contributions and encouragement.

And last, a very special thanks to Clarence Sr., Dorothy, Clarence Jr., Gerrie, Ray, Michael, Michelle, and Mark for their interest and enthusiasm.

Negotiations

1 Introduction

Many dictionaries state that to negotiate is "to confer, bargain, or discuss with a view to reach agreement." Negotiation may also be described as a "give and take" discussion resulting in a mutually beneficial relationship.

In reference to procurement, negotiation may be defined as the art of arriving at a common understanding through bargaining on the essentials of a contract such as delivery, specifications, prices, and terms. Because of the interrelation of these factors and many others, negotiation is a difficult art requiring judgment, tact, and common sense. The effective negotiator must be a real shopper, alive to the possibilities of bargaining with the seller. Only through an awareness of relative bargaining strength can a negotiator know where to be firm and where to make permissive concessions in prices or terms.

Negotiation occurs when two parties, each with its own viewpoints and objectives, seek to reach a mutually satisfying agreement in a matter of common concern. The process of negotiation involves:

1. Each party's presentation of its 'position,'—its concepts of the matter under negotiation, and its objectives.

2. Each party's analysis and evaluation of the other's position, to determine more fully strengths and weaknesses.

3. Each party's adjustment of its own position to reflect as much of the other party's views as it considers reasonable and justifiable. These adjustments may produce complete agreement between the two parties; if they do not, a final compromise by one or both parties may be necessary.

Successful negotiation requires that both parties be strongly motivated to reach agreement on the issue in question. If one party is not so motivated, agreement is possible only if the other party is willing to sacrifice completely its interests. Of course, this does not mean that the successful conclusion to a negotiation is always a fifty-fifty compromise between the parties or that a negotiated agreement where one party ultimately yields to the original position of the other is, by definition, inequitable. If the representative of one party concludes after thorough analysis that the total position of the other party is fair and in the best interest of both parties, his concurrence represents an equitable agreement.

1

In our society, negotiation is required, occurring at many levels to solve many problems. Nations oppose each other on various international issues. Labor and management negotiate problems of wages, hours, and conditions of work. Husbands and wives negotiate their own and other family problems. We negotiate with our children, and they negotiate with us. We negotiate with our supervisors to get and to keep a job. We negotiate with our peers for the cooperation and assistance necessary in the everyday business world, and we negotiate with our subordinates. In other words, negotiation is a far-reaching technique by which human beings with conflicting aims and objectives resolve those conflicts in an acceptable manner.

The importance of negotiation in our relationships with other nations cannot be overemphasized. For example, only to the extent that the United States and Russia can resolve the basic differences between their economic and political systems, will the world survive. If the two nations cannot negotiate, we may all perish. Of course, this negotiation is very difficult, for it is based not so much on factual differences as on ideological ones.

Regardless of the substantive nature of the issue, achieving a mutual agreement in the best interest of both parties is a result of many factors, including:

1. The equity of the aims and positions of each party
2. The clarity and completeness with which each party presents its own positions and evaluates that of the other party
3. The skill, experience, motivation, and open-mindedness of the two negotiators or negotiating groups
4. The willingness of both parties to compromise when a genuine impasse occurs
5. The relative power or bargaining positions apart from the facts of the situation of the two parties.

Though the material in this and succeeding chapters is oriented to the buyer-seller relationship, most of it also applies to personal relationships. The basic principles of negotiation apply to any negotiation: between governments, unions and management, buyers and sellers, or individuals. However, the material is directed almost completely to the negotiation of purchase orders and contracts between commercial firms.

Negotiation is generally thought of in terms of the initial pricing and settlement of contract terms and conditions. Actually, negotiation encompasses many more areas. In addition to the basic problem of determining a fair and reasonable price or return for manufacturing an item, commercial contracts have many provisions allowing the purchaser to make changes in the original terms and conditions of the contract that require negotiation of the equitable adjustments for such changes. In addition, negotiation is required in determining the interpretation and application of the contract terms and conditions.

The following is a general list of all areas in which the seller and the buyer must negotiate before the award or during the administration of a contract:

1. Price, terms, and conditions of the original contract
2. Contract interpretation after award
3. Adjustments with regard to the furnishing of commercial property, facilities, and special tooling
4. Changes in delivery points, drawings, and specifications, and the equitable adjustments for these changes
5. Variations in quantity
6. Determinations as to whether items meet the specifications and requirements of the contract
7. Price revision under redetermination, escalation, and incentive provisions
8. Problems about the acceptability of individual items of cost under cost type contracts
9. Negotiation of overhead rates for cost type contracts
10. Acceptability of accounting, inspection, and purchasing systems
11. The approval of "make or buy" programs and individual subcontracts
12. Negotiation of problems about the patent and technical data provisions of the contract
13. Termination settlements and problems about the disposal of property
14. Renegotiation problems where the seller may see the results of all his negotiation efforts in the basic contracts disappear.

We are concerned primarily with the negotiation of the original contract. However, the techniques of negotiation discussed apply equally to the negotiation of any type of an agreement necessary before, during, or after the period of contract performance.

During the term of a commercial contract, the seller may negotiate with the authorized Procurement Officer and the Cost Analyst, Legal, and Technical Personnel who assist him. During the performance of the contract, he may negotiate with the Administrative Procurement Officer, Auditors, Inspectors, Property Administrators, Security Representatives, and other Procuring Personnel concerned with the performance and administration of the contract. So, the seller is not dealing only with the "buyer" in the procurement process. He is also dealing with the Procurement Officer and the Procurement Officer's representatives. These representatives are individuals and have all the virtues and vices of other individuals. Nowhere else in commercial practice is a firm faced so substantially with the possibility that decisions by individuals will involve its welfare. There are many detailed regulations covering the procurement process. However, they establish only the broad limits within which the buyer and his representatives must operate. Within the regulations, the buyer's personnel have broad limits in which to exercise judgment.

During the initial selection of a seller to receive a contract, the regulations allow the buyer wide latitude in selecting the type of contract best suited to his interests. For example, a decision by the buyer that facilities or tooling necessary for the performance of the contract are special to the contract means that the buyer will pay for or provide the facility or special tooling. On the other hand, if the buyer determines—either in the initial contract negotiation for fixed price contracts or during the period of performance of a cost-type contract—that a facility or tooling is not special to the contract, then the seller must invest his own money in the item and charge the cost of that facility or tooling to his other business as well as to the buyer contract involved. This determination can represent thousands or even millions of dollars.

Many other examples emphasize the importance of negotiation in the procurement process, and the effect that adverse decisions can have on the welfare of the seller. These examples also emphasize that sellers must understand what is implied in the term "negotiation."

In procurement, the word "negotiation" has a specialized sense. It is not a process of giving in or of mutual sacrifice in order to secure an agreement. It is, rather, an attempt to find a formula that will maximize the interests of both parties. Broadly speaking, these considerations apply to all negotiations. However, they are tempered by the environment of the procurement and the particular problem being negotiated.

Some people consider negotiation as mere "horse trading." In many cases, because of lack of preparation or ability of the negotiators representing either the buyer, the seller, or both, negotiation does have many of the elements of "horse trading." Negotiation seems to be haggling or dickering as to what each side will accept. But professional negotiation is far more than that. It is not a process of mutual sacrifice for the sake of agreement: it is a method in which the buyer and the seller sit down and, by a specialized process of communication called "bargaining," reach agreement on the terms and conditions of the contract or settlement of the issue involved. This agreement reflects a balancing of the interests of the two parties over both the short and the long run.

There are many types of negotiation. In some cases, one side or the other will attempt to secure a settlement heavily weighed in its own favor by a blunt use of bargaining position. The buyer may do this if he finds out that the seller is extremely anxious to secure the contract. Sellers may do it when they are the sole source or selling a proprietary item. In this type of case, either side may assume an arbitrary, take it or leave it position. This is not true negotiation, and though it may lead to immediate short-range advantage, it generally ends in the development of hard feelings and retaliation at the first available opportunity. When sellers deal with a very limited market, a hard-nosed bargaining position is generally detrimental to their long-range interests.

Negotiation is the use of the techniques of persuasion and logical argument to convince the opposing side to agree with your position. It is designed not to win an argument but to resolve a complete problem. It is not a series of major battles over individual issues, because who wins an individual issue in negotiation is unimportant. The success or failure of either side in a negotiation depends on how the total difference of all the issues is resolved in a complete solution. In each case, the final solution must be considered in relation to its effect on the long-term relationship between the two parties.

Negotiation is a game like poker or chess; each game has a large element of chance, and generally the winner is the one who knows the rules, understands the psychology of the other party, is capable of both self-discipline and putting up a bold front, and is able to respond swiftly and correctly as opportunities develop during the conduct of the negotiation. Within the framework established by law and regulation, both sides have the right and, in fact, the obligation to attempt to make the very best deal they can for their own principals including, of course, the effect of their actions on long-term relationships with the other party. An intelligent negotiator will not take an extreme position, even if his bargaining position permits, since he may antagonize the other side, with resulting long-range losses. However, this decision should be based on strategic concepts, not on ethics. In the majority of cases, sound negotiation strategy is based on reasonableness; yet, the principal test of each move in negotiation is whether it is within the rules of the game.

Many sellers misunderstand completely the nature of negotiation and think that the buyer is questioning their integrity. The American business system normally operates on an offer-and-acceptance system in which items are sold at catalog prices or on a competitive basis. Businessmen are not accustomed to being asked to provide cost information or to substantiate it in negotiations. However, there are many situations in government and commercial procurement when competition is not possible, such as when:

1. Definitive specifications are not available
2. The work involves, for example, research and development, so that selection of a seller must be based on ability and experience rather than price
3. The seller is the sole source for either an initial or follow-on contract.

Normally in the private economy, price results from the interaction of complex forces. These forces are not always present in either government or commercial procurement, so negotiation takes their place. It may not guarantee a reasonable price, but it is the only substitute available.

Many businesses are fond of saying that their word is their bond. The number of lawsuits between businessmen indicates, however, that misunderstandings sometimes arise as to the interpretation of the "word." It is ridiculous to expect other people to take someone's word when large sums of money are involved and a conflict of interest is obviously present. If someone feels that his position is sound, he should be willing to explain and to defend it.

Many negotiators fail to understand the nature of negotiation, and so find themselves attempting to reconcile conflicts between the requirements of negotiation and their own senses of personal integrity. An individual who confuses private ethics with business morality does not make an effective negotiator. A negotiator must learn to be objective in his negotiations and to subordinate his own personal sense of ethics to the prime purpose of securing the best deal possible for his principals. A negotiator must understand the rules of the game in which he is engaged and must appreciate the fact that complete honesty is neither desirable nor practicable. In short, a negotiator must play to win. This does not necessarily imply that he should be ruthless, mean, or treacherous. On the contrary, a reputation for honesty and integrity is useful to a negotiator, because it improves his image, his relationship with the other side, and, therefore, his chances of winning.

Negotiation is an adversary action. In law, when a person pleads "not guilty" it is considered perfectly ethical for his attorney to defend him. Everyone recognizes that the function of the prosecutor is to convict and that the function of the defense is to defend. Both sides in a negotiation must recognize that they are in an adversary situation: within the framework of the law and given regulations and with due consideration for the long-range effects of their actions, they should play to win.

Henry Taylor, the British statesman, once stated that "falsehood ceases to be falsehood when it is understood on all sides that the truth is not expected to be spoken." In negotiation, it is necessary to tell the truth as one sees it, but not necessarily the whole truth. Many years ago, a business executive who was briefing his associates prior to their testifying before a government committee told them to "parry every question with answers which, while perfectly truthful, are evasive of bottom facts." Philosophers have been attempting for years to define "truth"; certainly, the negotiation table is not the place to find the meaning.

The comment of the Supreme Court concerning negotiation in the case of a buyer versus a major steel corporation is still valid after half a century. The buyer claimed that the seller made too much fee on a cost-plus-incentive-fee contract that had a fifty-fifty sharing formula. The buyer argued that "the contracts gave the seller the benefits of participating in the savings only if the seller, by special efforts, increased its efficiency and brought actual costs below the estimates agreed to in the contracts," and further argued that the contracts were invalid because the seller had used duress in getting the buyer to agree to the contracts. The Court denied both arguments of the buyer on the basis of the following statement:

The master found and the courts below agreed that the contracts resulted from negotiations in which both sides were represented by intelligent, well-informed and experienced officers whose sole object was to make the best trade possible under conditions which included the uncertainties of war time contingencies. The results from which, were not and could not have been known at the time the contracts were made.

2 Organization

The three primary attributes necessary for a person to be an effective negotiator are knowledge, attitude, and skill. Knowledge is the cornerstone upon which negotiation must be based. An effective negotiator must understand the product that he is buying or selling; he must understand the environment in which the procurement is taking place; he must understand the regulations covering the letting of government prime contracts and subcontracts or commercial procurements; and he must be completely familiar with business law, accounting, and pricing. The required knowledge covers the basic fields of engineering, legal, and business administration. Although individual specialists may be used effectively to support a negotiation, they can never replace a well-rounded individual able to understand and to interpret the problems associated with the entire procurement.

Next, the negotiator must possess the proper attitude toward, or philosophy of, negotiation. This involves a knowledge of his own psychology, the psychology of others, and the interaction of groups. Finally, an effective negotiator must be skilled in identifying the issues involved in a negotiation, in planning the strategy and tactics to resolve these issues effectively, and in communication, argument, and persuasion—the necessary attributes of the actual negotiation.

The man chosen to represent a company in contract negotiations should be acquainted with the broad details of the proposal, the item being manufactured, the method by which the cost information and price was developed, and the contingencies in the price. Whether or not the seller is successful in securing the price and the terms that he wants will depend to a great extent on the quality of the personnel to whom he assigns this important task. The person chosen must be able to plan and to execute his plans, and must be capable of controlling the members of his negotiating team. He must be a strong individual. However, "strong" should not be confused with stubborn, belligerent, or ruthless. A loud voice and the ability to pound the table are not the marks of a good negotiator. On the contrary, a loud-mouthed, aggressive individual always does more harm than good. Although the company negotiator must operate within the framework of procedures, policies, and ranges established for him,

9

he is not a mere messenger. He should have considerable freedom of action, because in dealing with the buyer he must be able to consider the various intangibles that enter into any negotiation.

It is important that the negotiator win the good will and respect of the buyer's personnel when he meets them. The person assigned by the seller to negotiate for him will make an impression that generally determines the buyer's opinion of the seller's organization. A good man can do a lot of good. A bad one can do a tremendous amount of harm. So a good negotiator needs a thorough understanding of his job, a keen feeling of responsibility, and above all else, a sense of courtesy. He also needs to understand his company, its product, and the regulations and criteria under which the buyer must operate; and he must fully appreciate the effect these criteria and regulations have upon the procurement in question.

He must be able to organize his team into an integrated, harmonious group, to plan his objective, and to explain his objective to the team members so that they will be able to coordinate their efforts most effectively to obtain the negotiation objective. He must know when and how to use specialists without being so narrow in his own understanding of the full complexities and ramifications of the procurement that he allows the negotiation to degenerate into a discussion amongst the specialists.

Besides knowledge, correct attitude, and skill, a good negotiator must have many other attributes.

1. He must be a clear, rapid thinker. The give and take of a complex negotiation requires a man who can think quickly.

2. He must communicate well. In negotiation, what you know is not so important as what you convey to others. The ability to express oneself clearly is an absolute must in negotiation. However, ease of expression should not be confused with glibness. Effective communication derives from a knowledge of the problem at hand and an acquired skill in negotiation.

3. He must be analytical and objective. He must be able to analyze the statements of others and to identify those that favor his position, those that oppose it, and those that favor another solution. He should be able to consider opposing points of view and the effects of these points of view on his own negotiation position.

4. He must be impersonal. In the heat of a hard-fought negotiation, it is sometimes very hard to control one's temper and to remain calm. But statements made in anger during a negotiation may plague the negotiator through the entire contract period, and, in some cases, may have extremely serious effects on the seller's future relations

with the buyer. The negotiator must always approach the negotiation from the basis of the company objective rather than from personal inclinations.

5. He must be patient. Sometimes an ability to let the other fellow talk himself out or explain his position fully pays dividends in resolving many issues without argument.

6. He must be able to consider the other person's ideas. He needs to see the frame of reference of the other side in order to evaluate their position.

7. He must be tactful, have poise and self-restraint, like people, and have a thorough knowledge of human nature.

8. He must have a sense of humor. The very fact that negotiation is involved means that you cannot win every point in a negotiation. An ability to make a concession yet continue to display good humor may produce sufficient good will to help resolve the remaining issues.

So, the effective negotiator rather than viewing himself and the technical, legal, fiscal, and other specialists as individuals with separate responsibilities, must regard himself as a captain or coordinator of a team of experts. He funnels information to them, evaluates their problems, avails himself of their skills. However, he should not transfer his responsibilities to them, because, in the long run, a successful negotiation requires broad knowledge covering all issues involved in the negotiation.

The variability of talent in negotiators in industry is very wide. They range from messenger, who merely transmits the unorganized individual contributions of the firm's technical, legal, financial, and administrative personnel, to the professional negotiators who understand all aspects of the procurement from the standpoint of both his own firm and the buyer. The latter has sufficient stature in the firm, either by position or by knowledge, to exercise fully the art of negotiation in the manner which is contemplated in the procurement process. His effective contribution will increase to the extent that he exceeds the minimum requirements. The more he prepares himself to take part in the entire procurement transaction, and the less dependent he is upon specialists in individual areas, the greater will be his ability as a negotiator, and the more valuable his contribution to his firm.

In selecting their representative(s) for a particular negotiation, some sellers try to consider a variety of factors, such as:

1. Individual personalities and experience
2. The desire to create an impression of interest on the part of top management

3. The desire to improve their bargaining position by using talkative negotiators to waste the buyer's time.

If a seller knows that he is in a sole source position and sure to get a proposed contract eventually, he may select stolid, resistant personalities to delay and to hold the line at the negotiation table, or he may not provide his negotiators with any authority to alter his firm's initial position. However, if he feels that his position is weak or unsound, a seller will probably select his most alert and aggressive personalities to try to take advantage of any opportunities that may arise during negotiation. Many sellers attempt to gain a psychological advantage through a show of force: that is, by having several members of top management such as the vice president, chief engineer, or sales manager represent them at negotiations.

The fact that the seller is represented by a team of top management personnel does not necessarily argue in favor of the buyer's countering with a team approach. Under certain circumstances, there may be a psychological advantage in not doing so. The seller's management may assume that the presence of a single negotiator means the pending procurement is routine and not urgent. However, although a negotiator may not actually work with a team at a particular negotiating session, he must have supporting specialists available if they are needed.

Often the buyer does not have the organizational flexibility to consider such factors as personality and bargaining position in assigning a negotiator to a particular procurement. As a rule, many procuring activities are organized on a commodity, commodity/contractor, or commodity/project basis. This permits individual negotiators to specialize in procuring similar items and equipment and often to deal with the same group of sellers over a long period of time. The resulting lack of flexibility can be a serious disadvantage. If a negotiator repeatedly uses the same techniques, arguments, and approaches in dealing with a seller, the seller may anticipate what will happen and be prepared to counter or to offset the buyer's position. This is particularly true of a buyer who always tries to reduce a seller's price by a given percentage. Knowing this, the seller simply inflates his quotation by a comparable amount, and the resulting price agreement bears no relation to the lowest reasonable price.

There is another argument for rotating personnel in procurement activity. Frequently, buyers who are assigned to work with the same seller for a number of years tend to "go native," becoming so familiar with the seller's operation and problems that they unknowingly develop a bias in his favor. This renders it impossible for them to represent properly the interest of their own agency or firm. Companies should watch for this possibility continuously: when any evidence of it shows, the personnel involved should be rotated to other assignments.

In assigning procurements to specific negotiators, both buyers and sellers should take into consideration experience and individual capabilities. It is generally sound practice to assign less complex, small dollar value, one-time, or CPFF procurements to less experienced personnel, and larger and more complex contracts to negotiators with greater experience. This is not an absolute rule, as a smaller procurement may have critical importance to either the buyer or the seller and, therefore, warrant top-level attention. The rule does not mean that smaller procurements create fewer and less difficult negotiation problems than larger ones do, or that less prenegotiation preparation is required for CPFF than for fixed price contracts. However, mistakes may be less costly in such procurement.

A major procurement action may involve many complex problems connected with accounting, pricing, legal, and technical areas. No individual could possibly be sufficiently knowledgeable in so many disparate fields. Even if such a person did exist, he would not be able to handle the entire job of preparing, planning, and executing a negotiation. The buyer recognizes this and backs up the purchasing personnel with a team of experts whose advice covers the entire procurement area. The team members include engineers, auditors, price analysts, lawyers, inspectors, buyers, and negotiators, all of whom are specialists in their particular fields.

The buyer is responsible for bringing to bear on the problem the expert knowledge of the best qualified personnel available. For example, engineers and technicians insure that the item to be procured is properly identified in the specification. They also assist in evaluating the bids or proposals received, to determine whether the items offered do, in fact, meet the requirements of the specifications. Auditors and price analysts are used to determine the reasonableness of offered prices or estimated costs. Lawyers advise on compliance with statutes and regulations and assure that the contract clearly expresses the intent of the buyer. Field personnel, in addition to the functions of inspection and contract administration, assist the buyer in determining the responsibility of prospective contractors.

Since the seller's personnel will be faced with a battery of specialists in particular areas, the seller should also use the team approach. The seller should be represented by a senior negotiator responsible for the outcome of the negotiation, assisted by as many kinds of specialists as are required for the problems anticipated in the procurement.

On both sides, team members are usually selected from the organization and have other duties and responsibilities. They may be inexperienced in the negotiation and may have trouble subordinating their individual personalities and specialties to the overall objective of the group. Therefore, the authority of the principal negotiator must be clearly defined. Negotiation is not a discussion between individual specialists. How one particular issue is resolved is unimportant, because the net effect of the negotiation is determined by the overall balancing of each issue involved in the negotiation process.

Team members must be aware of their individual responsibilities to advance the overall objective of the negotiation, even though they may have to sacrifice some professional opinions of their own. Specialists such as lawyers, accountants, and engineers tend to think in logical extremes. Negotiation is not a question of logical extremes, but rather an attempt to reach a reasonable agreement. For example, one negotiation bogged down in an argument between the price analyst for the government and the accountant on the contractor's team. The argument was a technical one involving an accounting procedure that, at most, would result in a net change up or down of $6,000 in the contract price. The principal negotiator called a recess and asked his accountant if he would give in gracefully on the argument, as the negotiator hoped that if the buyer gained a victory on this specific issue, he would take an easier approach toward the next issue on the agenda—which involved $84,000 in special tooling. But the accountant was determined to protect his professional status and was more interested in winning an argument than in advancing the team objective. The principal negotiator was finally obliged to order the accountant to concede the point or to leave the negotiation. With ill grace, the accountant conceded the point, and the principal negotiator was later able to reach an agreement that the buyer would absorb $75,000 of the $84,000 involved in the special tooling. Whether or not the principal negotiator's approach produced a favorable resolution on the issue of special tooling, it was a decision that only one person could make.

Negotiation teams are drawn from the various elements of the company organization, such as finance, engineering, manufacturing, and inspection. These team members may have organizational titles and stature on a level with or, in some cases, higher than the person chosen to represent the company. They must recognize, however, that negotiation is not an individual process, and that, in a well-integrated team, the overall objective of the negotiation always takes precedence over individual ideosyncrasies. The success of a negotiation team depends almost completely on the ability to achieve this integration. Team members accustomed to being leaders must learn to play supporting roles. The problem of the integration of team members is so great that a seller should seriously consider developing a permanent negotiation team or, at the very least, a hard core of personnel to represent the company, who will be supported by individual specialists as the need arises.

Before negotiations start, care must be taken that all team members fully understand their functions and know what they can and cannot do during negotiation. The subjects of team conduct and communication at the bargaining table should always be discussed fully in prenegotiation sessions. The negotiator should never assume that other members of the team will know how to act. Team members who are accustomed to leadership roles in their operating capacities may find it extremely difficult to play secondary or supporting roles at the negotiation table. They must be constantly reminded that the principal negotiator is the team leader. He is the spokesman, the only one who actually negotiates with the other side of the table.

The chief function of the other team members is to sit, to listen, and to evaluate. They participate in the conversation only when the negotiator specifically asks them to do so. If they are asked a direct question of substance by one of the representatives on the other side, they should be extremely careful before giving a direct reply. The safest procedure is to seek the negotiator's assent in some way before answering. When this is not done, communication controls break down quickly, and the negotiation position of the team is jeopardized. For his part, the team leader must know when and how to call on the members of his team and to use their skills to the best advantage. He must continually exercise the positive control necessary to insure effective communication and to exhibit a unified position to the other side.

If a team member forgets his role, becomes over-eager, and enters into an injudicious discussion with the other side, the negotiator must stop him. The negotiator should never hesitate to call a recess if he feels that he is losing control over the members of his team. If another team member feels that the negotiator has missed a vital point or has failed to take advantage of an opening that the contractor has inadvertently provided, he should keep silent until the next recess. A few missed opportunities are worth more than an undisciplined team.

However, recesses should be called with great care. The simple fact that a recess is called when a particular topic is discussed may provide the other side with a strong indication of the team's position on that issue. If a team member gets out of line, the negotiator should try to call a recess only after the subject under discussion has been dropped and another point brought up. Another method is to call for recesses at random, preferably during the discussion of a minor issue. These methods keep the other side in ignorance of the importance of any particular issue; and recesses called during the discussion of minor points may even serve to confuse them as to the importance attached to those issues.

There are two methods for training negotiators. The first, which is generally favored by many firms, permits the individuals to learn by actual negotiation. Ultimately, they become experienced enough to do an effective job. Of course, they usually have to use their experience with another firm, because the firms who use this method usually do not survive the training period. The second method is to train systematically the negotiators who will represent the firm in both buying and selling.

This training can be accomplished in a number of ways. First, the negotiator must acquire the broad technical, accounting, and legal background necessary to his company. Then he must have the opportunity to sharpen his negotiation skills by practice. This can happen in practice sessions, using negotiation problems in which the company or agency is currently involved. As part of the preparation for every negotiation, a team should be selected to represent the other side in a practice negotiation. This aids the preparation of actual negotiation and doubles as a training ground for neophytes. It also provides the firm with a method of evaluating their principal negotiators. Many firms have been shocked at the ineptitude displayed in practice by personnel responsible for major negotiations.

If the prospective negotiator displays the proper aptitude for negotiation in the training sessions, the next step is to assign him to act as an assistant to an experienced negotiator in real negotiation sessions. During this period, the trainee should continue to act in the practice sessions. Exposure to genuine negotiation should result in demonstrated improvement in his negotiation during the practice sessions. Later, the company should entrust the trainee with a small negotiation involving a small contract, or with a simple administrative problem on a larger contract. He should be accompanied by a senior negotiator experienced enough to bail him out if he gets into trouble and to evaluate his performance under fire. Gradually, as the trainee's skill and confidence increase, he should be assigned to larger and larger problems, until he can function without supervision.

This procedure may seem lengthy and expensive. However, it is not nearly so costly as using inexperienced negotiators. In no other procedure does so much money change hands based on the abilities of single individuals as it does in negotiation. In procurement functions particularly, a negotiator can make or break his company. He is the most important profit center the company has. He should be chosen, trained, and treated accordingly.

3 Psychology of Negotiation

Negotiation is conducted between individuals, either alone or supported by various technical personnel. The individuals at the negotiation table may be acquainted from past business dealings, or the negotiation may represent their first meeting. Regardless of whether or not they have known each other before, none of the individuals on either side will know too much about the background of the person with whom he is dealing. It is important to recognize that the attitude and approach brought to the negotiation table by every individual are affected by many factors unknown to the other individuals and perhaps unrecognized by the individuals themselves.

Each person at the table represents the sum total of his past background and environment. His home life, health, schooling, social life, ideas of right and wrong, and economic problems will all affect his attitude towards the negotiation. In addition, short-range private problems may completely change the person's normal personality. An otherwise affable representative of the buyer or seller may create serious problems simply because he had a fight with his wife on the day of the negotiation. Thus, a negotiator must recognize that sitting across from him is a complex individual affected not only by the environment at the negotiation table, but also by his personal history. He has pride, ambition, nerves, hopes, and status that will affect his attitude towards the negotiation. An effective negotiator must learn to recognize and to preserve these whenever possible.

The history and environment of each person at the negotiation table has a great deal to do with his "perception," defined as the process by which an individual receives or denies and interprets facts. This process is conditioned by his attitudes, opinions, emotions, temperament, character traits, and the many other psychological factors that affect human relationships.

An effective negotiator must first analyze himself. Then, in each negotiation, he must analyze his opponent. Remember that negotiation involves getting two extremely complex mechanisms with conflicting interests to compromise those interests. The first rule in negotiation is "Know thyself." The second is "Know thy opponent."

Negotiators representing both buyers and sellers come from a wide variety of backgrounds. Many have backgrounds in accounting,

17

law, engineering, or other educational disciplines. Normally, negotiators tend to concentrate on those areas of a negotiation in which
they have personal knowledge. The accountant will pay close attention to costs, the engineer to specifications, and the lawyer to terms
and conditions. To the extent that they concentrate on one area of a
negotiation, they may fail to do justice to other, more important areas.

Principal negotiators must be generalists. Although they may use
specialists to develop the details of their position on the many areas
involved in a negotiation, they must know enough to make appropriate trade-offs between various opposing interests, in order to
maximize their total position. Negotiators should carefully avoid a
tendency to concentrate their efforts in familiar areas and should
look for opportunities to exploit any evidence of this tendency on
the other side.

An attitude may be defined as a learned, rather set pattern of
thinking and acting about a given situation, circumstance, concept,
or individual. Because attitudes are derived from a person's opinions,
prejudices, and beliefs, they are emotional in nature. They are
learned by experience rather than by study or logical reasoning, and
so they are very difficult, sometimes even impossible, to change.

People tend to develop attitudes towards groups of other people
who are unlike them in either color, physiology, economic status,
religion, politics, or veteran status. These attitudes may manifest
themselves as active dislike, hatred, or fear of other people. Since
our subject is negotiation, not social psychology, we are concerned
with the impact that attitudes may have on negotiation. You cannot
negotiate with the devil; therefore, people who have strong attitudes
toward race, creed, color, politics, political systems, or economic
systems may find it extremely difficult, if not impossible, to engage
in effective negotiation, which invariably is based on some concept
of compromise.

The average American businessman does not understand procurement's role in establishing the environment in which his business
must operate. He tends to blame most of his difficulties on inter-
ference by buyers, failing to consider duly the help furnished by
procurement personnel.

Attitudes may arise from isolated or repeated experiences. For
example, a seller who must continuously deal with an untrained,
unmotivated purchasing employee, will eventually develop the
attitude that all purchasing employees are stupid and unmotivated.
Similarly, if a buyer does business with a limited number of sellers,
all of whom seem to be in business solely to make a profit without
considering their contribution to national defense, he may develop
the attitude that all sellers are venal or outright crooks.

Once an attitude is established, isolated or even repeated different experiences do not necessarily lead to the development of permanent new attitudes, if they are in conflict with the older, more deeply seated ones. Once individuals develop their initial attitudes, they tend to look for incidents that substantiate their attitudes and to ignore things that disprove them. Even when the basis for an attitude is explained, the person involved usually denies it or refuses to believe it. Some even rationalize that their attitude is the right one.

Since attitudes are by definition illogical, they have no place at the negotiation table. After first checking themselves to insure that they are capable of making the determination, senior management for both sellers and buyers should check out each negotiator carefully to insure that he has the necessary objectivity and emotional stability to participate in negotiations.

To be effective, a negotiator must explore his attitudes towards the other side and its representatives, he should attempt to correct extremely adverse attitudes or, at least, to keep them under control so that they do not interfere with the progress of the negotiation.

Opinions are a temporary way of perceiving something. They are less deeply rooted than attitudes and are generally based on a more intelligent analysis of the problem. People are generally aware of their opinions but may not be aware of attitudes. The broader a person's background, the more intelligent he is, and the wider his experience, the less apt he is to develop deeply rooted attitudes.

Emotions are inner feelings or disturbances which lead to overt bodily reaction. They are important for the enjoyment of life, reaction to environment, and their effect on other beings. People tend to be conditioned by their emotions.

Emotions either cause or are triggered by bodily reactions to a particular environment. The most important response is made by the adrenal gland, which is activated by fear or by a threat to the security of an individual. The adrenalin it releases can cause many changes to the body: heartbeat increases, blood pressure rises, respiration increases, the chest expands, digestion slows or stops, the nervous system is alerted, the pupils of the eye dilate, the liver releases sugar into the blood, and the clotting time for blood decreases. These changes were programmed when the threat to human security was physical; when our ancestors left their caves for their family's lunch, they were very likely to encounter an animal such as a saber-tooth tiger bent on the same errand. In many cases, who was whose lunch depended to a great extent on the rapidity of response to danger.

This same physiological response occurs when we encounter present-day threats to our security. Happily, these threats exist not in the form of actual physical violence, but are our business failures or successes. This is particularly apparent in negotiation, so it is important to keep in mind that these responses may occur and to recognize that they tend to distort our mental processes. We must also use these mental processes, figuratively speaking, to spear our opponent across the negotiation table.

Individuals who react emotionally when they are opposed or placed under stress should be kept out of negotiations. Calculated emotionalism has a place in negotiation. Glandular problems do not.

Temperament is defined as the individual peculiarity of physical organization by which a person's manner of thinking, feeling, and acting is permanently effected. It is his natural disposition. There are considerable differences in temperament among peoples. Some are active and cheerful, others querulous, and yet others phlegmatic. These differences, commonly lumped together under the term "temperament," together with the intelligence of a person, are innate and possibly hereditary.

Some people do not have the type of temperament suited for negotiation. Because negotiation involves dealing with people, it requires an understanding of human nature. A person who, by temperament, dislikes other people and is uncomfortable in their presence cannot make an effective negotiator unless he can understand and match his temperament to the requirements of the negotiation process. Some people are introverts, concerned chiefly with their own activities and own thoughts. Since effective negotiation requires the ability to delve into the thoughts of others and to recognize, even to anticipate, their reactions to various positions and issues within the negotiation process, an introvert must develop an objective ability to direct his interest outside himself. In other words, he must develop some of the qualities of an extrovert. Extroverts, on the other hand, may have to tone down the more extravagant facets of their personalities.

At this point, we should distinguish among opinions, attitudes, and character traits. Opinions are a temporary way of perceiving something and are likely to reflect current public feeling. We are all familiar with the ups and downs of the opinion polls at election time. In many cases, opinions reflect what a person thinks he should feel rather than what he does feel. Opinions are easily changed and are usually subject to either logical argument or to propaganda.

Attitudes, however, are normally deeply rooted and do not necessarily reflect public opinion, although they do reflect the opinion of the group or groups with which an individual associates. Ordinarily, attitudes are associated with character traits that lead a person to select from the hundreds of things impinging on him those which agree with his basic attitudes. Character traits are developed early in life, so they are very difficult to change. However, character traits combined with personality and attitudes, though rigid, can also allow for considerable variation in behavior. For example, a person who dominates his inferiors and submits to those whom he considers his superiors is not necessarily showing contradictory attitudes: they both stem from his respect for authority. An individual who is shy under certain circumstances, and self-assertive in others, is not necessarily contradictory: the individual may feel a strong need to impress people, displaying confidence in those areas in which he is informed and shyness in others. Psychological research has shown that prejudices are not based solely on individual attitudes towards specific situations, circumstances, concepts, or other individuals, but rather may reflect an entire method of thinking about the world in which a person lives and his specific relationship to it.

Psychologists have developed strong statistical confirmation of what is described as a radical-conservative factor. The right-wing or conservative attitude results from submission to a dominant father figure, and hence to substitute father figures met throughout life. A person with this attitude respects power and authority even if the respect is often confused. On the other hand, the radical attitude results from freedom to rebel against the father figure or its substitute in the external world. It stems from an ability to adopt a child's standpoint as opposed to the parents', or the standards of one's own ego as opposed to those of the group.

The most important of these corelated and contrasting conservative right versus radical left attitudes may be listed as follows:

	Conservative		*Radical*
1.	Loyal to a single father figure or leader	1.	Loyal to group
2.	Upholds family	2.	Suspicious of family
3.	Stresses discipline in relation to education, penology, etc.	3.	Stresses freedom
4.	Antifeminist	4.	Feminist
5.	Stresses sexual restraint	5.	Stresses sexual freedom
6.	Patriotic	6.	Cosmopolitan
7.	Upholds class distinctions	7.	Tends to classless society
8.	Upholds conventions and traditions	8.	Critical of conventions and traditions
9.	Upholds religion	9.	Antireligion
10.	Upholds private property	10.	Socialistic
11.	Prejudiced	11.	Unprejudiced

These political attitudes refer to fundamental emotions and should not be confused with the political programs of individual political parties. In the majority of cases, no person, except for extremists on the left or right, would fall completely into one group. The majority tends to group somewhere around the middle, with the extremists at either side.

Basic character traits tend to assist in the formation of attitudes, which are usually developed at a very early age, becoming so fixed that they are almost personality traits. Once established, these attitudes are very difficult to change, because they are part of an integrated personality pattern which cannot be altered piecemeal. Weaker attitudes are functions of the groups to which a person is related, and so the only way to change the individual's attitude is to change the attitude of the group.

Trying to alter an individual's attitude by direct argument is the most difficult approach of all: in effect, you must imply that he was wrong to start with. He will automatically accept this as a personal attack and will, therefore, become doubly resistant to change. Research has also shown that the stronger the attack on the personality, the more resistant the person is to change. The more conservative the other negotiator, the more careful you must be not to contradict him directly. You must contrive to win your points without making it seem that he is losing his.

Quite a number of years ago, it was discovered that all of us go through daily emotional cycles during which our emotions fluctuate within narrow ranges from a feeling of well-being to a feeling of depression. The daily cycles contribute to a longer emotional cycle that varies within individuals but that, on an average, covers a six-week period. During this period, the individual starts out at a low point, rises to a peak of well-being, and then descends to a low point from which the cycle will commence again.

This cycle is physiological in nature. It is, of course, complicated in its daily and longer period fluctuations by individual incidents. For instance, the daily cycle may be complicated by health, by isolated conditions in the environment, or by lack of rest. This basic emotional cycle must be understood because, in many cases, it provides an explanation of behavior that would otherwise be inexplicable with respect to personality and temperament changes at different periods of time by different people. It is useful in understanding the reactions of both superiors and subordinates; and it explains much about negotiation, where personal relationships play such an important role. If you realize that the average human being is controlled as much by his glands as by his head, you will expect and be prepared for unpredictable behavior.

In a study of domestic chickens, psychologists discovered an interesting phenomenon. If six hens are placed in a barnyard, they immediately establish an order of rank, which psychiatrists label the "pecking order." Hen number one is entitled to the preferred position at a feed trough with hens number two, three, four, five, and six quickly establishing their own rank. The same phenomenon has been identified in other birds and animals.

The pecking order is also present, although not quite so obviously, in human relationships. Thankfully, humans attempt to establish relative rank and position by subtler means than simply pecking other people on the head. The most common human manifestation is expressed by the statement "keeping up with the Joneses." Many people attempt to establish rank or economic position by outward manifestations of their wealth, such as houses, cars, boats, clothes, travel, specific colleges for their children, and other means.

The concept of the pecking order is very common in business relationships. The type, location, and furnishings of an office are usually a good indicator of the relative position of an executive in the hierarchy of a company. When a company has an executive dining room, who sits at which table is established by his rank in the organization. At the chief executives' table, rank determines not only who sits there but also which chair he sits in. The closer to the "throne," the more important the person. Once, when invited to sit at the chief executives' table in a major company, the author sat down at the president's right hand, preempting the executive vice president's place. It would have been funny, if it were not so tragic to see grown men milling around like chickens defending their places at the feeding trough.

Attempts to establish a pecking order can also be identified in the majority of negotiations. For example, sellers will often be represented by the president, vice president, or general manager of the firm. His position in their organization is generally superior to that of the buyer's negotiator. This difference in position may have a psychological effect on the buyer, unless he keeps in mind that at the negotiation table, the principals are equal. The results of a negotiation are determined by the bargaining position and skill of each side.

During the negotiation, each side may attempt to establish the general pecking order. For example, the buyer may request information about the type of improvement curve used by the seller to develop the labor hours used as the basis for his quotation. Then, if the seller admits ignorance of the improvement curve, the buyer explains in a condescending fashion the principles behind the use of an improvement curve. Of course, this tactic may backfire: for example, the seller may immediately begin a discussion of the advanced concepts of the use of an improvement curve, thus exposing the fact that the buyer was unfamiliar with the concepts.

Another method used by many negotiators is to try to overpower the other side by shouting or by other evidences of aggressive behavior. This approach can be offset in a number of ways. You can attempt to outyell the other side; this makes an amusing, if not necessarily constructive, negotiation. Another way to handle a person who talks loudly and aggressively is to whisper at him or to ask him if he is deaf. Yet another response is to call a recess with the announced intention of moving the negotiation session to a sound-proof room because the loud talker may disturb the functioning of the rest of the organization.

Since humans will be humans, it may be assumed that in the initial stages of a negotiation, each side will attempt to feel out the abilities and responses of the other side and to establish superiority by either knowledge, vocal strength, or other means. This period, though expected, should be short if professionals are involved.

Another factor that must be considered in negotiation is the differences between "strong" and "weak" personalities. Some individuals are strong, aggressive, and determined. Others are relatively easygoing and permissive. The use of the terms "strong" and "weak" in this regard does not imply that strong is necessarily better than weak, especially where negotiation is concerned.

A successful negotiator should understand his own personality, his strengths and weaknesses, and adjust his approach to the specific problems of the particular negotiation. For example, if the bargaining position is clearly on your side, perhaps the best strategy would be to assert your position forcefully. On the other hand, long-range considerations may temper your approach so that you present a relatively weak position to the other side of the table. Conversely, if your position is extremely weak, it may be necessary for you to balance this actual weakness with a strong, determined stand on the particular issue. Or, when faced with a weak situation, you may be wise to admit the weakness and, in effect, to throw yourself on the mercy of the other side. (This would, of course, depend upon the personality on the other side of the table.) The majority of us like to help people if we can.

Regardless of your personal inclination, to be effective as a negotiator, you must learn to subordinate your basic personality characteristics to the needs of the particular procurement.

An introvert is someone who directs his interest or attention to himself. Conversely, an extrovert is a person whose interest lies more in his environment and in other people than in himself. An introvert tends to be shy, while an extrovert is normally active and expressive. Much has been written about the differences between introverts and extroverts; however, usually every human being is a combination of both. An extrovert is often an introvert who has overcompensated.

Without going into a detailed clinical analysis of the differences between the two basic types, perhaps stereotypes may be used to identify them. An extrovert may be personified by the movie concept of the Texas rancher with a big ten-gallon hat, flamboyant clothes, and back-slapping, loud-mouthed personality. On the other hand, an introvert may be personified by a precise, impeccably dressed banker. Some psychologists have suggested that the way to identify the two types is by their manner of dress, the preciseness of their conversation, and the manner in which they approach a problem. However, appearances may be deceiving. The impeccably dressed banker may dress that way because it is expected of him during business hours, while off-duty he asserts his true personality in the flamboyant dress of the extrovert. Conversely, a person with the facade of an extrovert may actually be deeply introspective.

In negotiation, an extrovert tends to wheel and deal, while an introvert tends to negotiate each issue exhaustively. An introvert is normally interested in detail, while an extrovert is bored with too much trivia. Certain negotiation techniques, particularly those involving pressure, may work on extroverts but would be resented by introverts. Since personality is such an elusive thing to define, perhaps the best advice that could be offered is to analyze yourself. Determine whether you are more introverted than extroverted, or vice versa. Then determine which types of approach appeals to you and which do not.

An effective negotiator must recognize and control his attitudes, opinions, emotions, physiological responses, and emotional cycles to the extent that they color and distort his objective approach to a negotiation. He must understand that the same responses and problems are present in the persons with whom he is negotiating. They may, in turn, recognize these responses, or they may be ignorant of them. The negotiator may use the attitudes, emotions, opinions, and responses of others to his own advantage, but should never allow others to take advantage of his.

4

Bargaining

The first step in preparation for any negotiation is the evaluation of the relative bargaining or power positions of the buyer and the seller. Bargaining power may be defined as the relative strength or weakness of one party's total position, which effects his will or need to compromise in reaching agreement with the other party. Such strengths and weaknesses may result from many factors, both tangible and intangible, such as:

1. The number of qualified firms competing for a contract
2. The urgency of the seller's desire for a contract
3. The amount of time the buyer or seller has in which to seek an agreement
4. The accuracy of one party's assessment of the other's negotiation objectives, and the facts and estimates that support these objectives
5. The external pressures—regulatory, legal, political, public, and so forth—that one party can use to force agreement from the other
6. The accuracy of one party's evaluation of the other's bargaining position.

The relative bargaining position of the buyer and the seller in a particular procurement is perhaps the most important single determinant of which side will "win" the negotiation. However, relative bargaining position is not necessarily a factual condition. Bargaining position comprises two elements: the objective bargaining strengths of both sides, and the relative skill of the negotiators on both sides of the table.

In negotiation, the strongest party does not always win, and the outcome does not always reflect the relative bargaining position of each side. Many factors affect the outcome of a negotiation, and a settlement is reached only when a number of factors equaling the minimum positions of both sides are agreed to. In negotiation, it is assumed that each side wants to reach an agreement; however, the minimum terms acceptable to each side may prevent an agreement from being reached regardless of how interested both parties are in reaching that agreement. So, negotiators on both sides should make every attempt to improve their own positions, both in prenegotiation preparation and during the actual negotiation. The goal of negotiation strategy is to maximize one's own bargaining position at the expense of the other party.

Unfortunately, many negotiators fail to understand the nature of negotiation. They feel that because their position is supported by facts, logical persuasion at the negotiation table will automatically result in the other negotiator's seeing the justice and rightness of their position. In so doing, they fail to consider the possibility that the other negotiator probably has exactly the same attitude towards his initial position. Nothing is worse than a negotiation conducted by two self-righteous negotiators, each completely assured of the justice, correctness, and ethics of his own position.

The major factor affecting the bargaining position of the buyer and the seller is the amount of competition present in the procurement. Normally, the use of maximum competition is required by law in government procurement and should be the goal in commercial procurement as well. If a prospective seller knows that other firms have been invited to compete against him for a specific contract, his offer will reflect this fact. He will try to price his offer low enough to eliminate his competition but high enough to allow for his profit or whatever other benefit he is seeking from the contract. When competition is present, therefore, normally the buyer is assured of receiving the lowest price available from the suppliers he solicits.

Even in procurements in which the lowest price is not the specific objective, such as research or development contracts which are generally awarded to firms that have the highest competence in a specific branch of science or technology, procuring maximum competition from qualified firms provides the buyer with the greatest advantage and relative bargaining position possible. If the seller feels that he may lose a contract to a competitor, obviously he will be far more amenable to compromise or to minimize most of his procurement objectives (especially price), assuming that he really wants the contract.

Unfortunately or fortunately, depending upon one's viewpoint, a significant percentage of negotiations often involve limited or sole source situations. While in some cases a seller does not know this and the buyer should do everything possible not to reveal it, often a seller is aware of the lack of competition, so his bargaining position will improve greatly.

A seller's need or desire for a particular contract is another factor that may affect the relative bargaining position of the two parties. The buyer can determine this feeling in a number of ways.

If the contractor's sales or profits have been falling off in the past accounting period, or if his current backlog, translated into future production time, is low, the negotiator may have an indication of the firm's need for additional business.

On the other hand, a large dollar backlog does not necessarily indicate that the prospective seller cannot perform the work in time to meet the buyer's delivery requirements or that he is not anxious to obtain the work. He may have excess capacity in certain of his departments that is not reflected in the total backlog: all of the contractor's activities are not involved in one procurement at the same time. There is a flow of work through various departments such as engineering, tooling, plant setup, production, inspection, packaging, and shipping. In order to maintain his business properly, the seller must continually start new projects to keep this work load at a level and his personnel gainfully employed.

The industry in which a particular seller works or the organizational structure of his firm may also provide insight into his need and desire for a particular contract. The size, sales volume, or backlog of the current concern notwithstanding, it is more than likely that a division specializing in government contracts will be eager to secure more. Another factor improving a buyer's bargaining position is that the divisions of many large firms have charters restricting them to individual areas such as space, electronics, or underwater development. This limits the number of contract opportunities available to them. At the same time, the corporate management expects them to compete vigorously to maintain the division's position, within the limited sphere prescribed in their charter.

Another criterion applicable to the seller's need or desire for a particular contract is the nature and amount of work to be performed. Obviously, the larger the order and the longer its duration, the more important it becomes to the seller who receives it. The same is true of orders that lead to follow-on work or to commercial advantage or that will improve the seller's position in the industry. Commercial advantages may range all the way from a direct benefit for a firm's commercial products to the intangible benefits of institutional advertising.

There are two types of pressure that handicap the buyer: delivery schedule pressures (lead-time pressures), and administrative pressures. As a rule, time pressures work to the seller's advantage and the buyer's disadvantage. The chief exception to that occurs when the seller has a small backlog or is operating at less than full capacity and therefore needs the additional work badly.

Urgent delivery dates coupled with irreducible production lead-time often put pressure on the buyer and may strongly effect his bargaining position if the seller is aware of the pressure. In some cases, the use of a letter contract to get the work started may be the only solution to this pressure for a specific procurement. However, this is an unhappy solution, for it greatly enhances the seller's subsequent bargaining position.

Restrictive lead-time also decreases the buyer's chances of securing competition for a procurement. Over the long run, improved procurement timing and the earlier release of procurement requests are the only solution to the delivery problem. Unfortunately, the premature release of purchase requests can present a serious drawback, because it increases the incidence of changes to the Request For Proposal before award and to definitive contracts after award.

Administrative pressures that reduce the buyer's bargaining position arise from many sources:

1. The buyer's total work load
2. The need for obligating funds as the end of the fiscal year approaches
3. The unfortunate fact that too many supervisors evaluate individual buyers on their ability to conclude agreements in the shortest possible time with a minimum of trouble.

Some of these factors can be minimized if the buyer is more selective in expending his time and effort, some by a change in philosophy on the part of management, and some by improved procurement planning and work load scheduling.

In most cases, sellers are aware of the time pressures working on a buyer and formulate a negotiation strategy or employ delaying negotiation tactics to maximize this advantage.

There are many external pressures—legal, regulatory, political, and public, and so forth—that one party or the other may invoke to enhance its bargaining position. Many factors work to the buyer's potential advantage, including:

1. Company-established policies, developed for procurement personnel, establish the framework within which buyer negotiators must operate and set down rules as to what they may or may not do.

2. The buyer negotiator's need to obtain approval of most negotiation agreements.

3. The existence of other review agencies such as the Defense Contract Audit Agency, the General Accounting Office, and the Renegotiation Board.

4. The buyer's status as the largest single buyer in the world, and the seller's awareness that his actions in one procurement may influence his ability to secure future government business.

5. The weight of public opinion against the contractor who attempts to take advantage of the government, wasting taxpayer's money and jeopardizing the nation's defense effort.

6. The activities of congressional investigating committees, which have not been adverse to pillorying contractors in the court of public opinion.

Factors that may strengthen the seller's bargaining position in a given situation include:

1. The pressure exerted by political groups to secure government or other business for their constituents.

2. The pressures sometimes exerted by engineering groups to have a specific contractor perform the desired work. In some cases, the pressures are justified, if one contractor is, in fact, the most qualified to perform the work. In others, however, the pressures may reflect prearranged agreements that are detrimental to the buyer's interests.

3. The pressures of precedents favorable to the seller, if he has been able to secure concessions from the same or other government agencies or private companies on past contracts.

4. The pressure of company policy, generated, for example, by a refusal to do business on other than a fixed price basis.

5 Estimating Cost Ranges

Estimating involves the exercise of a great deal of judgment. The estimator is trying to determine what costs should be at some point in the future. This implies some type of projection of current experience into the future, or adjustment of a current standard for a future production environment. It is rarely sufficient to apply costs of one period as the estimate for another period, without adjustments. The manner in which these adjustments are made is the major judgment in the cost estimate. For example, judgment may require an estimated increase in material prices or labor rates during the performance of the proposed contract. But these potential increases may be offset by reductions in labor hours based on the "learning" of employees, improvement in processes, tooling, and facilities, and reductions due to increases in quantity requirements. In other cases, firms may make arbitrary reductions or increases in estimated costs based on their analysis of what the competition will do and what the traffic will bear.

Different firms necessarily prepare their estimates in different ways, and the same firm may prepare different types of proposal in different manners. Some of the more common methods of estimating found in industry include round table, comparison, and detailed.

In round-table estimating, representatives of interested departments such as engineering, manufacturing, contracts, purchasing, and accounting may be brought together to develop the costs from experience, knowledge of the product, and knowledge of market conditions. The estimate developed by this method is usually completed without benefit of detailed drawings or bills of material and with very limited information concerning specifications. Usually, standard costs are available for a large percentage of the parts. This type of estimating has the advantage of speed and is relatively inexpensive.

Estimating by comparison usually involves the estimator and representatives of the interested departments. A characteristic is selecting a guide from comparable parts or processes whose costs are known. Complexity factors are then developed, and elements of material and time are deleted from or added to the known costs as necessary to make the new product. This method is often found where requirements for the new product are very similar to those for a past or existing product and where relatively few adjustments need be made in producing the estimate.

Detailed estimating is characterized by a thorough, detailed analysis of all components, processes, and assemblies. This type of estimating determines labor, tooling, material, and additional capital item requirements. The application of labor rates, material prices, and overhead or burden to the calculated requirements translates the estimate into dollars. Detailed estimating is further characterized by the presence of complete calculations, records, and quotations that remain available for future use.

To perform detailed estimating, the estimator must separate each component into parts, operations, and cost elements. The data used include drawings, bills of material, specifications, production quantities, production rates, analysis of manufacturing processes, tooling and capital costs, machine and work station workloads, plant layout, manufacturing, engineering and tooling labor, raw material and purchased parts, overhead, special tools and dies, and factors such as labor efficiency, labor learning, setup, rework and material scrap, waste, and spoilage.

The usual procedure is to have each department that is involved in the proposed program submit estimates of the number of direct labor hours, both hourly and salaried, and the cost of raw materials, purchased parts, subcontracted items, tooling, facilities, and other direct expenses required for performance if the contract is secured. In large companies, individual estimates may be developed by as many as twenty engineering departments, ten manufacturing departments, three or four test or tooling departments, and various service departments. Many times, these estimates bear little or no relation to the expected cost of performance.

The complexity of the problem may be such that no reasonably accurate cost estimate is possible. Lack of properly trained estimators within the departments may make it impossible or difficult for the department manager to come up with a realistic estimate. In other cases, where an accurate estimate is possible, individual department managers may inflate or deflate the estimate based on their own budget and personnel usage problems. Pricing may consist of nothing more than applying standard overhead and bidding rates to the raw cost data from the departments and adding the totals. Furthermore, in many cases management will increase or decrease the figure depending on their judgment as to what the traffic will bear.

Regardless of the system, prime costs will be estimated, using historical actual cost data on this or similar items, standard cost data on this or similar items, or the personal judgment of qualified technicians. Usually the estimate is a combination of all three systems. The key is to remember that the estimator is trying to determine what costs should be at some point in the future. The various factors applied to the prime costs are either labor-rate applications to labor hours or overhead applications to both labor and material costs. Both of these require detailed analysis by the estimator to establish the conditions that will exist when the prime costs are incurred.

Labor-rate projections involve analysis of the local and regional economic trends as well as the national trend. These data will reveal the underlying trends affecting labor as a whole. The other parameter is the mix of labor in the specific company considered. Information is needed on the growth (or decline) forecasted in the labor force during the period of production and on how the mix of labor will change either by category or plantwide, whichever rate is being projected. Rate charts showing the actual labor rate by month and either the head count or manhours by month over a past period are helpful.

Overhead factors will vary from allocations of fixed costs on some logical basis to allocation of variable costs on specific base costs. Charts plotting the past actuals and the related base costs are usually the best and easiest method of evaluation and provide a basis for projection. These costs correlate so closely with prime costs that they must be evaluated together. Indirect labor, for example, is a major part of most factory and engineering overhead pools. Plottings of indirect-direct labor ratios are the most helpful in projecting indirect labor in a future period. Correlation is the key here.

Most of these rates and factors are applied mechanically to the prime costs by the estimating group, although some estimating groups will monitor the realism of the rates and factors. As a general rule, the rates and factors are applied by direction received in the form of rate letters either from management or, through management, from the department concerned.

In most companies, the cost estimate is subjected to management review before release to sales and eventual use as support for a proposal. The objectives of this review are to obtain the commitment of the operating groups to operate within the estimate, to apply profit objectives, and to determine the salability of the price, considering competition, past prices, how much the buying agency has to spend, the corporate image, and other similar factors. In many instances, the cost estimate is changed arbitrarily in this review. This sort of action may be based on management decisions such as:

1. On a CPFF proposal, take a lower cost to stay within the buying agency's budget figures
2. In a competitive, firm fixed-price situation, lower the price to obtain or retain business
3. Lack of confidence in ability to produce within the estimate.

No amount of estimating skill on the seller's part, cost and price analysis on the buyer's part, or conscientious negotiation can arrive at an exact determination of the cost outcome of a project. Even the most routine production work can be affected by unforeseen shifts in labor rates, material prices, or economic conditions. An estimate is a prediction of future events, so it will inevitably contain some degree of uncertainty, some probability that a contract completion cost will be, for example, five, ten, or twenty percent above or below the initial estimate. Negotiation, then, is concerned not with a single cost but with a range of possible cost outcomes. Normally, the narrower this range, the more willing the seller is to accept the risk on a fixed-price basis.

The purpose of the seller's estimating process and the buyer's price and cost analysis is to develop some idea of the possible range of costs within which the contract work may be performed. The extent of this range from minimum to maximum, factored by the bargaining position, will determine the type of contract used and therefore the relative cost risks of the contract to both parties (see Figure 5-1).

Establishing the range of possible costs is not easy. Since the estimate is just that, an estimate, conclusions about its accuracy can be no more than similar estimates. The following factors will provide guidelines as to the nature of contract.

1. The nature of the work. In general, a high ratio of development to fabrication will tend to create a higher degree of uncertainty. It will be helpful, therefore, to isolate the various cost elements and assign levels of uncertainty to each one. Raw materials, routine purchase parts, drafting labor, and so forth would normally carry relatively low uncertainty levels. Testing labor, on the other hand, may be assigned a high uncertainty, because one or two major test failures could double the amount originally estimated for this category. Engineering labor, too, must be analyzed on the basis of the work to be performed. For example, the amount of such labor engaged in redesign or reconfiguration of proven hardware may be

		firm fixed-price confidence limit ± 5%
$95,000	$105,000	

		fixed-price-incentive confidence limit ± 5% to 20%
$95,000	$120,000	

		cost-plus-incentive-fee development confidence limit ± 20% or more
$80,000	$140,000	

cost-plus-fixed-fee R&D
no confidence in cost-completion form; no confidence in scope-term form

?   ?   ?   ?   ?   ?   ?   ?

Figure 5-1. Cost-Price Analysis

considered relatively certain and controllable. Conversely, engineering labor engaged in more demanding state-of-the-art work may carry a high degree of uncertainty.

2. Past experience. In situations where both the seller and the buyer have had little experience in estimating costs on similar work, confidence in the negotiated target is normally low. The same will be true when past experience does exist but the accuracy of the estimates was limited.

3. Negotiation environment. If the initial position of the two parties is relatively far apart, one or both is likely to have little confidence in the final price. This is especially true if either party believes the other has based his negotiation primarily on bargaining position.

4. Time available. The degree of confidence in target costs will increase substantially if adequate time has been made available for careful estimation and thoughtful negotiation.

When confidence limits are finally estimated, they are first used as indicators for the appropriate contract type. In general, when the upper limit is less than ±10%, the buyer should concentrate on negotiation of a firm fixed-price arrangement. For an upper limit between 10 and 20% the fixed-price-incentive (FPI) is usually appropriate. When confidence decreases to a level beyond + 20–25%, it is usually necessary to shift to the cost-plus-incentive-fee (CPIF) form. Thereafter, the CPIF is appropriate, at least theoretically, regardless of the deterioration of the confidence limit level. However, as the confidence limits widen, the CPIF share becomes smaller and approaches a cost-plus-fixed-fee (CPFF) arrangement, in which case the administrative cost and problems associated with the administration of the CPIF may not be worth the incentive provided by the small share.

It is important to recognize that a good estimate represents a good estimate at a point in time, so it will change with time; that an estimate is not absolute but is only a point in a range of possible actual costs; that this range of costs establishes the negotiation positions of both parties; and that the actual price established in a negotiation will be established on the basis of the relative strengths and weaknesses of the two parties.

6 Cost Data Usage

Negotiation is used when it is not possible to establish a price by competition. When negotiation is contemplated, the buyer normally asks for information concerning the cost elements that the seller proposes to include in his price. In procurement, there are requirements that prospective contractors and subcontractors submit cost or pricing data under certain circumstances.

The requirement that cost or pricing data be submitted in negotiated procurement has been in the ASPR since the first edition of 1948. As a result of reports to the Congress by the General Accounting Office which alleged overpricing by government contractors, in 1959 the ASPR was revised to require all departments to obtain a Certificate of Current Pricing. In 1961, the ASPR was amended to provide for the inclusion of a defective pricing data clause giving the government a contractual right to reduce the contract price if it was later determined that the price was overstated because of defective cost of pricing data. Despite these requirements, a number of reports by the GAO indicated that unreliable cost or pricing data were still used in price negotiations.

In 1962, Congressional concern led to the enactment of Public Law 87-653, known as the "Truth in Negotiations Act." ASPR was revised to include a new Certificate and Defective Pricing Data Clause. In addition, for the first time a clause was inserted to provide for an audit to determine the accuracy, currentness, and completeness of the cost or pricing data that formed the basis of the contractor's proposal. The Federal Procurement Regulations (FPR) have also been amended to make the requirements applicable to all government agencies.

The cost or pricing data requirements of the law are stated briefly in five basic provisions:

1. Prime and subcontractors shall be required to submit cost or pricing data.

2. Prime and subcontractors shall be required to certify that the cost or pricing data submitted are accurate, complete, and current.

3. The requirements for prime and subcontractor submission is made applicable to awards or transactions expected to exceed $100,000.

4. Where certification is obtained, a provision for price reduction shall be contractually incorporated to permit adjustment of the established price to exclude any significant amounts by which the price was overstated because defective cost or pricing data were submitted.

5. Last, the requirements for submission and certification of cost or pricing data need not apply in cases where the price negotiated is based on adequate price competition or established catalog or market prices of commercial items sold in substantial quantities to the general public, prices set by law or regulations, or in special situations where a Secretarial waiver is obtained.

The emphasis on cost or pricing data has led many contractors and contracting officers to forget the reason that data is required in the first place—namely, to negotiate a price, target price, or cost estimate. This emphasis is based on the assumption that estimating is an exact science rather than an art and implies a static condition in the contractor's business operations and the economics of the country that is not present in real life. The assumption seems to be growing that negotiation is an exercise in accounting rather than an exercise in business judgment by both sides.

To refute this, a detailed review of DOD pricing and negotiation policy, based on excerpts from the regulation and a DOD letter to the Comptroller General, is furnished below.

Case 1 of this chapter, "Cost Data Usage In Negotiation," is designed to illustrate how the application of different standards of judgment can result in different price objectives (see Figure 6-1). A detailed comparison of the reasons for the wide range between the seller's and buyer's position is provided. The case illustrates how two parties may prepare their negotiation positions and the type of argument used.

To illustrate Case 1 further, consideration should be given to the following pricing policy. Insofar as costs are concerned, the buyer and the seller start from their separate understandings of two things: cost experience relevant data showing what it has cost in the past to accomplish tasks comparable to the contract work, and forecasts of what it should cost to perform the contract which are generally

seller's projected unit costs for 1000 units	seller's actual historical costs for production of 200 units	buyer's projected unit costs for 1000 units
$140.99	$82.20	$51.00

Figure 6-1. Price Objective Differences

based in large part on projections of the relevant cost data in the light of contingencies which may affect future costs. The first is essentially factual and is normally based on the contractor's cost or pricing data, which has to be current, accurate, and complete. The second is essentially a matter of applying judgment to the possibility of various contingencies occurring and involves recognizing the degree to which these contingencies will be within the control of the buyer, the seller, or neither. In most cases, the first depends heavily on the seller's books and accounting records, which reflect past costs by individual cost elements; if the books and records accurately reflect costs in a way that will not mislead is the proper concern of accountants and auditors. The second depends not only on cost trends and projections based on past costs, which concern accountants and auditors, but also on assessments of how risks should best be distributed between seller and buyer, how much potential there is for reducing costs by controlling contingencies, and how pricing can best be used to exploit this potential—assessments that call for judgments outside the normal sphere of accountants and auditors on matters that cut across individual cost elements and may be entirely unrelated to any specific cost element.

When cost experience is involved in price negotiations, we expect our negotiators and the contractor to reach a mutual understanding of facts on each significant cost element. In this area, as noted above, we are concerned with facts rather than judgment. There is no intrinsic reason for the parties to differ on what costs have been experienced or on how these costs should be distributed to individual cost elements. But the situation is very different for forecasts of what it should cost to perform the contract concerned. Here we are concerned with judgment—not facts. There are intrinsic reasons for the parties to differ on how to provide for contingencies—reasons as valid as they are elementary. On one hand, we expect our negotiators to work toward a negotiation objective that requires maximum effort by the contractor to earn a fair profit; our negotiators will tend to minimize contingencies. On the other hand, the contractor will tend to maximize contingencies and to work toward a negotiation objective that reflects his fear that most, if not all, unfavorable contingencies will become realities before contract performance is complete. Thus, we do not expect our negotiators to agree with the contractor's forecast, nor him with ours, but rather that both forecasts will be founded on the same factual basis. We also expect that both parties will bargain in the understanding that the total of all forecasts is a sum of possibilities—not certainties—and that compromise of extremes may be necessary to a fair settlement.

Responsibility of Pricing Personnel

Occasionally, differences of opinion exist not only about the reasonableness of cost projections but also about the accounting techniques on which they are based. In addition, it is usually impossible to negotiate a pricing result in strict accord with all of the opinions of all of the specialists, or even with the buyer's pricing objective. Reasonable compromises are necessary, and this fact must be understood by all members of the team. For all of these reasons, audit reports or pricing recommendations by others must be taken as advisory only. The buyer is responsible for exercising the requisite judgment and is solely responsible for the final pricing decision. In those instances when the buyer does not adopt audit or other specialist recommendations that have particular significance for the contract price, he should include appropriate comments in the record of the negotiation.

Relationships of Cost, Profit, and Price

Where products are sold in the open market, costs are not necessarily the controlling factor in establishing a particular seller's price. Similarly, where competition may be ineffective or lacking, estimated costs plus estimated profit are not the only pricing criteria. In some cases, the price appropriately may represent only a part of the seller's cost and may not include an estimate for profit or fee, as in research and development projects where the contractor is willing to share part of the costs. In other cases, price may be controlled by competition. The objective of the buyer is to negotiate fair and reasonable prices in which due weight is given to all relevant factors.

Profit or fee is only one element of price and normally represents a smaller proportion of the total price than do other estimated elements such as labor and material. Although the buyer wants to avoid excessive profits, he should not become so preoccupied with particular elements of a seller's estimate of cost and profit that the most important consideration, the total price itself, diminishes in significance. Procurement is concerned primarily with the reasonableness of the price that the buyer ultimately pays, and only secondarily with the eventual cost and profit to the seller.

Pricing Data or Cost Defined

Cost or pricing data as used in the case study (see page 000) consists of all facts existing up to the time of agreement about price that prudent buyers and sellers would reasonably expect to have a significant effect on the price negotiations. The definition of cost or pricing data embraces more than historical accounting data; where applicable, it also includes factors such as vendor quotations, non-recurring costs, changes in production methods and production or procurement volume, unit cost trends such as those associated with labor efficiency, and make-or-buy decisions or any other management decisions under the proposed contract. In short, cost or pricing data consist of all facts that can reasonably be expected to contribute to sound estimates of future costs as well as to the validity of costs already incurred. Cost or pricing data are factual and can be verified. Because the seller's certificate pertains to "cost or pricing data," it does not make representations about the accuracy of the seller's judgment as to the estimated portion of future costs or projections. It does, however, apply to the data upon which the seller's judgment is based. This distinction between fact and judgment should be clearly understood.

Basic Considerations

Under fixed-price contracts, the negotiated price is the basis for payment to a seller, whereas allowable costs are the basis for reimbursement under cost-reimbursement type contracts. Accordingly, company-established policies and procedures are governing and are followed in the negotiation of fixed-price contracts. Cost and accounting data may provide guides for ascertaining fair compensation but are not rigid measures. Other data, criteria, or standards may furnish reliable guides to fair compensation. The ability to apply standards of business judgment as distinct from strict accounting principles is the heart of a negotiated price of settlement.

Among the different types of fixed-price contracts, the need to consider costs varies considerably, as indicated below:

1. **Retrospective Pricing and Settlements.** In negotiating firm fixed prices or settlements for work that has been completed at the time of negotiation (e.g., final negotiations under fixed-price-incentive contracts, redetermination of price after completion of the work, or negotiation of settlement agreement under a contract terminated for the convenience of the buyer), the treatment of costs is a major factor in arriving at the amount of the price or settlement. However, even in these situations, the final price or settlement may represent something other than the sum total of acceptable cost plus profit, since the final price accepted by each party does not necessarily reflect agreement on the evaluation of each element of cost, but rather a final resolution of all issues in the negotiation process.

2. **Forward Pricing.** The extent to which costs influence forward pricing varies greatly from case to case. In negotiations covering future work, actual costs cannot be known and the importance of cost estimates depends on the circumstances. The buyer must consider all the factors affecting the reasonableness of the total proposed price, such as the technical, production, or financial risk assumed, the complexity of the work, the extent of competitive pricing, and the seller's record for efficiency, economy, and ingenuity, as well as available cost estimates. He must be free to bargain for a total price that equitably distributes the risk between the seller and the buyer and provides incentives for efficiency and cost reduction. In negotiating such a price, it is not possible to identify the treatment of specific cost elements, because the bargaining is on a total price basis. Thus, while cost data is often a valuable aid, it will not control negotiation of prices for work to be performed, or a target price under an incentive contract.

Use of Cost Data
in Negotiation

One of the Electrospec Company's major products was galvanometers, which it sold to prime contractors, upper-level subcontractors, and to commercial firms. On November 1, 1967, the Air Force requested a proposal on 1,000 galvanometers identical to a new model, 200 of which had been previously sold only to the Avion Electric Company, a major prime contractor. The galvanometers had been sold to Avion Electric Company for $150.00 each. The Federal government requested that cost and pricing data be submitted, including a DD Form 633. The seller had just been through an audit relating to the establishment of a negotiated final overhead rate for the previous year for use on its cost-type contracts. The seller also had accurate information concerning labor and material costs available from the previous procurement.

On the first proposal to Avion Electric, the seller had included a burden rate of 157%. Because of a reduction in business, the most recent audited manufacturing burden rate was 212.6%.

The "Customer Service Expense" audited rate was 2.55%; however, the auditor had disallowed approximately 75% of these expenses, including advertising, salaries, commission, and expenses in connection with the salesmen.

The "General and Administrative Expense" audited rate was 8.06% after the auditor had eliminated contributions, patent expenses, credit and collection expenses, and bad debts amounting to $15,600.

Using these rates, the total unit cost on the previous contract was only $82.20.

Considerable discussion occurred among the members of the management of the company when it came to pricing the proposal for 1,000 units. Discussion centered on the following major points:

1. The galvanometer was a new improved model. The Air Force had requested the RFP. Within reasonable limits the company could assume that it was a sole source.
2. The volatile nature of the company's business prospects because of the effects of World War I on the Defense budget.
3. The fact that all economic indicators forecast strong inflationary pressures on wages and prices.

After analyzing these factors, plus the cost projections furnished by the financial department, the company submitted a price of $140.99 per unit.

After receipt of the seller's proposal, the auditor reviewed the seller's cost records for manufacturing the original 200 galvanometers. He found that the costs were as stated but disagreed completely with the seller's projections. After reviewing the auditor's comments and the seller's proposal, the negotiator and price analyst came up with a unit price objective of $51.00 per unit.

Comparison of Seller's Price and Buyer's Price Objective With Previous Actual Unit Costs

	Seller's Cost Projection	Previous Unit Costs	Buyer's Cost Projections
Purchased Parts[a]	$ 1.67	$ 1.529	$ 1.46
Other Raw Materials[b]	3.11	2.834	2.92
Direct Labor[c]	24.45	22.281	12.80
	(11.7 hours @$2.09)	(11.7 hours @$1.904)	(6.4 hours @$2.00)
Manufacturing Overhead[d]	69.82	47.369	22.37
	(285.6%)	(212.6%)	(182.6%)
Packaging[e]	0.34	0.310	0.34
Subtotal	$ 99.39	$ 74.323	$ 40.89
Cust. Serv. Expense[f]	13.44	1.895	1.10
	(13.4%)	(2.55%)	(2.7%)
G&A Expense[g]	9.75	5.990	3.55
	(9.8%)	(8.06%)	(8.7%)
Subtotal	$ 122.58	$ 82.208	$ 45.54
Profit[h]	18.41		5.46
	(15%)		(12%)
Price	$ 140.99		$ 51.00

Seller's Position

[a]Based on previous actual unit cost of $1.52 plus a 10% increase. This increase is based on the seller's prediction of increased prices due to the copper strike, recent inflationary price increases in steel, and wage increases in the automobile industry.

[b]See above.

[c]Direct labor hours are based on previous actual unit costs. Labor rates of $2.09 per hour are based on actual labor rates for previous production of the same item factored by a 10% increase projected at the estimated midpoint of the effort of the proposed work. The estimated 10% wage increase follows the contractor's prediction of increased costs based on an

Buyer's Position

[a]This 5% overall reduction is based on the buyer's assumption that an increase in quantity from 200 to 1,000 should result in a substantial reduction (10% or more) on some of the purchased parts. Taking into account possible inflationary increases, this averages out at 5% overall.

[b]This is a 3% increase in recognition of possible material increases. Taking into account that the contractor will be able to order the material immediately upon the award of the contract, the buyer considers this an adequate contingency.

[c]The labor hours are based on the previous actual unit costs extended through 1,000 units on an 80% improvement curve. The $2.00 per hour rate is based on the historical rate factored by a 5% increase, which recognizes the possibility of a wage increase.

48

analysis of the recent inflationary wage increases granted in the automobile industry, and statements by national union leaders that they intend to press for high wage and fringe benefit increases.

[d]The manufacturing overhead rate is based on the contractor's projection of increased overhead costs and decreased labor during his current fiscal year.

[d]The manufacturing overhead rate is based on the assumption by the buyer that the contractor's volume will remain approximately the same. Indirect labor and certain other costs are factored for possible increases. Certain design engineering costs are deleted. No design engineering is required by the contract; therefore, the buyer does not believe these costs are allocable.

Calculation of Manufacturing Overhead Increases

1. Mfg. O.H. Last Year

Salaries & Wages	$173,136
Other Overhead	178,293
Total Mfg. O.H.	$351,429

2. Projected Mfg. O.H. Current Fiscal Year

Salaries & Wages	$190,499 (173,135 + (10% increase)
Other Overhead	187,207 (178,293+ (5% increase)
Total	$377,656

For explanation of assumptions on which increases are based, see Notes (a), (b), and (c).

3. Labor Base $132,216

Labor base for current year based on contractor's projection of a 20% decline from his previous fiscal year base of $165,270 in the amount of direct labor based on a decline in business and a change in labor-material mix of his contacts.

4. Projected Overhead Rate Based on A, B, and C.

Mfg. O.H.	$377,656
Direct Labor	132,216
Mfg. O.H. Rate	285.6%

Calculation of Manufacturing Overhead Increases

1. Mfg. O.H. Last year

Salaries & Wages	$173,136
Other Overhead	178,293
Total Mfg. O.H.	$351,429

2. Projected Mfg. O.H. Current Fiscal Year

Salaries & Wages	$173,136 − 46,309 (Engr. costs) $126,827 + 6,341 (5% increase) $133,168
Other Overhead	183,641 (178,293+3%)
Total	$316,809

A 5% increase in allocable overhead salaries and a 3% increase in other costs is provided for.

3. Labor Base $173,533

This is based on the buyer's assumption that the contractor's labor base for the current year will be essentially the same as the previous year's $165,270 plus 5% for expected wage increases.

4. Projected Overhead Rate Based on A, B, and C.

Mfg. O.H.	$316,809
Labor	173,533
Mfg. O.H. Rate	182.6%

Seller's Position (cont.)

[e]See Notes (a), (b), and (c).

[f]1. Total customer service expense = $88,902. This rate derives from a projection based on contractor's total customer expense of $81,391 for the last fiscal year plus an estimated 8% increase in these costs, which consist primarily of labor.

2. Projected material base for current fiscal year $151,956. This increase is based on a projected 10% increase in material costs [See Notes (a), (b), and (c)] and an estimated 10% increase in material usage due to expected change in the mix of work. [This is consistent with projected drop in direct labor. See Note (d).]

3. Projection of cost of goods manufactured for current fiscal year

Material Costs	$151,956
Labor Costs	132,216
Mfg. O.H. Costs	377,656
Cost of Goods Manufactured	$661,828

4. Calculation of projected customer service expense rate

Cust. Serv. Exp.	$ 88,902 (=13.4%)
Cost of Goods Manufactured	$661,828

[g]This rate is based on a projection of the total G&A expense for the last year of $60,516 (including the $8,600 disallowed by the auditor), adjusted for salary increases and projected changes in the allocation base.

1. Total G&A last fiscal year

Labor	$ 33,523
Other	26,993
Total	$ 60,615

2. Projected G&A current fiscal year

Salaries & Wages	$ 36,875 (33,523+10% increase)
Other	28,342 (26,993+5% increase)
Total	$ 65,217

Buyer's Position (cont.)

[e]No comment.

[f]1. Total customer service expense = $16,746. This is based on the amount of customer service expense accepted by the auditor for the previous year ($16,391) factored by a 5% increase for the labor portion ($7,083 × 5% = $354.15).

2. Projected material base for current fiscal year $130,429. This is based on the buyer's assumption that the contractor's material costs for the current fiscal year will be the same as for the last fiscal year, with the addition of a 3% factor to cover possible material increases.

3. Projection of cost of goods manufactured for current fiscal year

Material Costs	$130,429
Labor Costs	173,533
Mfg. O.H. Costs	316,809
Cost of Goods Manufactured	$620,771

4. Calculation of projected customer service expense rate

Cust. Serv. Exp.	$ 16,746 (= 2.7%)
Cost of Goods Manufactured	$620,771

[g]This rate is based on the total G&A for the seller's previous fiscal year of $51,916 factored for expected increases. Buyer does not include $8,600 disallowed by the auditor for the seller's previous fiscal year on the basis that the items do not contribute to and therefore should not be allocated to this contract.

1. Total G&A last fiscal year

Labor	$ 33,523
Other	18,393
Total	$ 51,916

2. Projected G&A current fiscal year

Salaries & Wages	$ 35,119 (33,523+5%)
Other	18,945 (18,395+3%)
Total	$ 54,064

Seller's Position (cont.)	Buyer's Position (cont.)

This is based on the buyer's assumption that the contractor's G&A costs are composed primarily of fixed costs that will remain the same regardless of output.

3. Calculation of G&A rate

Projected G&A Expense	$ 65,217
	= 9.8%
Projected Cost of Goods Mfgd.	$661,828

3. Calculation of G&A rate

Projected G&A Expense	$ 54,064
	= 8.7%
Projected Cost of Goods Mfgd.	$620,771

[h]15% of total costs based on Weighted Guidelines.

[h]12% of total costs based on Weighted Guidelines.

Appendix 6-A

Following is a listing of the audited Material Costs (Schedule I), Manufacturing Overhead (Schedule II), Customer Service Expense (Schedule III), and General and Administrative Expense (Schedule IV):

Schedule 6-1: Material Costs

Material Costs (Year Ending 6/30/59)	$126,630

Schedule 6-2: Manufacturing Overhead

Year Ending 6/30/59	*Adjusted Totals*
Salaries and Wages	
Supervision	$ 31,326
Clerical	24,239
Other Indirect	53,006
Manufacturing Engineers	14,471
Engineers	46,309
Other	3,785
Overtime Premium	4,606
Night Bonus	1,470
Holidays and Vacations	21,774
Factory Supplies	16,169
Engineering Supplies	3,181
Perishable Tools	5,153
Maintenance	12,572
Engineering Travel	2,547
Telephone & Telegraph	2,444
Power and Light	3,400
Group Insurance	7,057
Pension Provision	3,754
Payroll Taxes	5,459
General Insurance	2,484
Property Tax	12,685
Scrap	5,495
Depreciation	62,572
Engineering Building Occupancy	1,842
Professional Services	387
All Other Factory and Engineering Expenses	3,242
Total	$351,429
Direct Labor	$165,270
Manufacturing Overhead Rate	212.6%

Indirect Expenses: The totals include provision for anticipated increases of 5% indirect wage and salary rates, vacation pay, depreciation due to new plant and equipment, and so forth. They also include anticipated decreases in property taxes, professional services, and so forth.

51

Schedule 6-3: Customer Service Expense

Year Ending 6/30/59	*Adjusted Totals*
Salaries	
Administrative	$ 7,083
Clerical	4,142
Traveling	2,738
Building Occupancy	
Other	1,994
Total	$ 16,391
Cost of Goods Manufactured	
(Material + Labor + Mfg. O.H.)	$643,329
Customer Service Rate	2.55%

Customer Service Expenses: The instrument portion has been reduced approximately $65,000 by the auditor for items classified as not allowable. These include commissions, advertising, salary and expenses of the salesmen, and so on.

Schedule 6-4: General and Administrative Expense

Year Ending 6/30/59	*Adjusted Totals*
Salaries	
Administrative	$ 15,033
General Accounting	11,906
Cost Accounting	6,584
Supplies	1,840
Traveling	1,158
Postage	859
Professional Services	5,030
Building Occupancy	1,127
Payroll Taxes	1,429
General Insurance	1,771
Depreciation	1,368
Building Allocation	3,811
Total	$ 51,916
Cost of Goods Manufactured	$643,329
G&A Rate	8.06%

General and Administrative Expenses: Items eliminated from this classification of accounts totalled $8,600 for contributions, patent expenses, credit and collection expenses, and bad debts.

7

Planning (Seller)

In preparing for negotiation, the most pressing problem for the seller is insuring that a negotiation will take place. When the seller submits his proposal, theoretically he bases it on his best analysis of the environment of the procurement in which the proposal was made. In many cases, however, the seller prepares his proposal in too little time to do an effective job. Many companies send a proposal in on the due date, breathe a sigh of relief, and wait for the best or the worst to happen. This procedure is based on several fallacious assumptions: the seller has done the best job he is capable of doing in the preparation of the proposal; he fully understood all the requirements of the Request For Proposal; he was responsive to all the requirements of the Request For Proposal; the proposal is presented in such a manner that the buyer can determine that it is responsive to the Request For Proposal; the seller can neither change nor add to his proposal after it is presented.

In procurement, it is important to remember that until the contract is signed by the buyer and returned to the successful contractor, there is a possibility that the buyer will change his mind. Therefore, regardless of how far ahead of the competition the company thinks it is at the time initial proposals are presented, it may lose the contract. Likewise, regardless of how poor the seller's proposal seems initially, there is always a chance that with the proper approach and follow-through, a poor proposal can be turned into a successful contract. Consequently, the seller's first step after a proposal is submitted is to contact the buyer to discover if the proposal is responsive to the Request For Proposal and if there is any additional information that the buyer needs.

These are standard guidelines for Request For Proposal reviews. After receipt of initial proposal, written or oral discussions should be conducted with all responsible bidders who submit proposals within a competitive range, price, and other factors (including technical quality, where technical proposals are requested) considered, except that this requirement need not necessarily be applied to:

1. Procurement not in excess of $2,500
2. Procurements in which prices or rates are fixed by law or regulation

3. Procurements in which time of delivery does not permit such discussions
4. Procurements of the set-aside portion of partial set-asides or by small business restricted advertising
5. Procurements in which it can be clearly demonstrated from the existence of adequate competition or accurate prior cost experience with the product or service that acceptance of the most favorable initial proposal without discussion would result in a fair and reasonable price.

In the latter, however, the request for proposals should notify all bidders of the possibility that award may be made without discussion of proposals received, and hence that proposals should be submitted initially on the most favorable terms from a price and technical standpoint that the bidder can submit to the buyer. In any case where the pricing or technical aspects of any proposals are uncertain, the contracting officer should not make award without further exploration and discussion prior to award. Further, when the proposal most advantageous to the buyer involves a material departure from the stated requirements, consideration should be given to offering the other bidders an opportunity to submit new proposals on a technical basis comparable to that of the most advantageous proposal, provided that this can be done without revealing to the other firms any information that is entitled to protection. Guidelines provide that a seller submitting data that he does not want disclosed to the public or used by the buyer for any purpose other than evaluation of the proposal may legend the proposal and restrict its dissemination.

Whenever negotiations are conducted with more than one seller, auction techniques are strictly prohibited; for example, the buyer may not indicate to a bidder a price that must be met to obtain further consideration, or inform him that his price is not low compared to that of another bidder. On the other hand, it is permissible to inform a bidder that his price is considered by the buyer to be too high. After receipt of proposals, no information regarding the number or identity of the bidders participating in the negotiations should be made available to the public or to any one else whose official duties do not require such knowledge. Whenever negotiations are conducted with several bidders, successively or otherwise, all sellers selected to participate in such negotiations should be offered an equitable opportunity to submit any price, technical, or other revisions in their proposals that may result from the negotiations. All such bidders should be informed of the specified date (and time, if desired) of the closing of negotiations and that any revisions to their proposals must be submitted by then. All such bidders should be informed that any revision received after such date will be treated as a late proposal in accordance with the "Late Proposals" provisions of the Request For Proposals. (In exceptional circumstances, when the buyer authorizes consideration of such a late proposal, resolicitation should be limited to the selected sellers with whom negotiations have been conducted.) Additionally, all such sellers should be informed that after the specified date for the closing of negotiation, no information other than notice of unacceptability of proposal, if applicable, will be furnished to any seller until award has been made.

An important procurement upon which the company has expended a great deal of preproposal and proposal effort should be carefully monitored to insure that any changes in the procurement environment will be picked up and appropriate changes in the company's approach or proposal made to counter them. Close contact should be maintained with the procurement and technical personnel of the buyer until the contract is signed or a "Business Won Or Lost" report is prepared.

Though a lazy buyer might prefer to take the proposals, evaluate them technically, and then pick the lowest priced proposal from the acceptable technical proposals, this is not efficient purchasing. Some proposals may have been developed by poor proposal writers or by firms that misunderstood the requirements. It is to the buyer's advantage to insure that the "Request For Proposal" was understood, and then to consider the best deal offered. It is difficult to determine if the lowest quotation is the best possible that can be obtained under the circumstances. A buyer should assume that the seller's initial proposal is his maximum proposal and that he will reduce his price if given the chance.

In cases where he is a sole source, the seller knows that his proposal will eventually reach the negotiation stage. In a competitive procurement, however, the seller is not necessarily assured that his proposal will be negotiated unless he himself takes the initiative. In some cases, the problem is relatively easy. The buyer will request that negotiations start. In other cases, a pre-award or facility survey will be made. This does not always indicate that the seller's proposal is being considered or is the best; but is a sign pointing in that direction. However, when a firm has been doing business continuously with the service or prime contractor involved, a formal pre-award or facility survey may not be made.

In many cases, the only recourse is to go in and ask. The regulations state that the buyer is not supposed to tell the seller whether or not he is being considered or the number or identity of other bidders. Some buyers are more skillful at withholding this type of information than others. The ability of the buyer to keep the seller in doubt about his position is one of the buyer's principal bargaining strengths. Yet many buyers do not realize this, or do not seem to care, and will provide the seller with information about his competitive position. In other situations, the technical personnel involved in the procurement will provide the seller with the information he wants. In extreme cases, they may even provide information about buyer's objective in the procurement or the amount of money available. If this information can be secured, it provides a valuable bargaining tool for the seller. Even if the buyer follows the regulations and refuses to give the seller any information, his attitude or the manner in which he greets the seller may provide the seller with some indication as to where he stands.

The seller should exercise all legitimate means to determine if his proposal is being considered. If he determines that his proposal is *not* being considered, he should take immediate steps to decide where the proposal is deficient. If the problem is that he has been, in effect, "lapped" technically, there is probably nothing he can do about it. But if he is acceptable technically, and the difference lies only in the cost proposal, then the seller should examine the marginal effects of decisions for and against a reduction sufficient in amount to make his proposal acceptable. Making a reduction during the prenegotiation stage represents a very delicate problem.

In many cases, a good buyer will attempt to create an impression in the seller's mind that a price reduction is in order. For example, in one procurement agency the buyer's desk was located immediately adjacent to the elevator. Unknown to each other, two contractors competing for the same procurement were in the building. Contractor A got off the elevator and greeted the buyer with a questioning look. Since he was the low bidder and the buyer expected to be negotiating with him in the near future, the buyer smiled encouragingly. Reassured, Contractor A went about his business in the building. Shortly thereafter, Contractor B got off the elevator, gave the buyer the same questioning look, and was met with a blank stare. Recognizing the symptoms, Contractor B went into a corner, recalculated his bid on the spot, and submitted another offer, which he promised to reaffirm in writing. The original Contractor A then came past the buyer's desk again on his way out of the building. He smiled at the buyer and the buyer looked at him with a blank look. A skillful seller experienced in the ways of procurement personnel, Contractor A realized that his competitive situation had changed. He went over to the corner, recalculated his bid, and promised to reaffirm it by letter as soon as he returned to his firm. The buyer laughed and said to his nearest neighbor, "Well, that was an easy procurement. By simply raising my eyebrows, smiling, or looking blank, I just saved the company over $200,000."

This does not usually happen in such rapid sequence, and so obviously, but it does happen often enough in procurement. After the proposal is presented, it must be continually monitored through to a successful conclusion.

The seller's preparation for negotiation actually involves his entire proposal effort. He should recognize that if his proposal is not complete or if items are not properly explained, particularly in the cost area, these points will most likely arise during the negotiation. So, it is not a question of whether or not the information will be provided, but when.

It is important that the principal negotiator and his team members be completely familiar with the development of the proposal. The proposal team should analyze the competition, trying to anticipate the information that they will request or the questions they will ask. One method is to re-examine the proposal, prior to negotiation, from the standpoint of the buyer and to look for holes that may lead to questions from the buyer.

It is important that the negotiating team know how much technical and pricing analysis of the proposal occurred. Often, auditors, price analysts, and technical personnel will come in to a seller and analyze a particular area of the seller's proposal. Each one will provide the buyer with a memorandum covering the results of his visit. In many cases, the negotiation team may not be aware of the extent of the analysis, the caliber of the people involved, the areas in which the most interest was displayed, and the problems that arose from the interview. Each person contacted by any representative of the buyer should immediately summarize the results of the interview and give a copy to the negotiation group for their review and analysis.

The next problem is to review the strengths and weaknesses of the seller's negotiating team and the buyer's team. Make sure that your team is well organized, technically competent, and that the authority and position of the team leader is clearly understood by each member of your team. Base your analysis of the buyer's team on past dealings with them or on inquiries to others within your organization who have dealt with them in the past. Then, appraise objectively the relative bargaining positions and strengths of both sides. The seller's bargaining strength depends on:

1. How much he needs or wants the contract
2. How sure he is that he will get the contract
3. How much time is available to reach agreement
4. The organizational and personal status of the seller.

The buyer's bargaining strength depends on:

1. The amount of competition present
2. The adequacy of the cost or price analysis
3. How much the buyer needs the seller
4. The relative profitability of the contract
5. How much time is available to reach agreement
6. The organizational and personal status of the buyer.

In analyzing any procurement situation, you must recognize that many of the problems inherent in the procurement are outside the control of a single person or even a group of individuals. Failure to recognize this may lead to serious negotiation problems. Success in negotiation does not stem from striving for logical extremes but from doing the best that can be done considering the circumstances and environment of the procurement. In analyzing the competition, it may be assumed that prices will be based as much on the seller's estimate of what the competitors' prices will be as on what his own estimated average costs are. Therefore, the negotiators for both sides must estimate the effect that other bidders have had upon the proposals received. But note that the number of bidders does not necessarily represent the yardstick by which competition is measured. There may be keener competition among three sellers for a prized contract than among twenty.

In many proposals, of course, price or estimated costs is not the principal criterion, so firms spend their major effort in developing the technical and management proposal, adjusting if necessary, their cost estimate to meet the amount of money available for the procurement—which may have no relation to the actual amount of effort spelled out in the proposal.

Even a sole source situation does not necessarily lack competitive aspects. A sole source producer is restrained from too great a use of his bargaining position by the fact that the buyer may establish a second source or switch to a competitive item. In effect, the possibility of future competition may provoke some current, if limited, competitive restraints.

The seller should also evaluate the buyer's known behavior patterns or attitudes, if they will affect the negotiation. Some buyers favor cost-type contracts; others, fixed-price contracts. A buyer who exhibits this type of favoritism pays little attention to the selection of an appropriate type of contract based on the developments of the bargaining situation. Instead, he commits himself in advance to a specific form of contract and restricts his negotiation to an attempt to beat down the seller's price. Many buyers have established a pattern of insisting on a minimum of five, ten, fifteen, or twenty percent reduction in the seller's initial proposal. Once this type of behavior has been identified, negotiation becomes simple, for all the seller needs do is quote a price or estimated cost high enough to allow the buyer to take out his percentage yet still leave the seller with the amount he desired in the first place.

The personal qualifications of the buyer should be analyzed: his knowledge and skill in negotiation, and also the strengths or weaknesses he has revealed in previous negotiations. Some buyers operate on the principle that the seller is attempting to defraud them. Other buyers, particularly those who have had a long, continuous relationship with the same seller, sometimes "go native" and become more aware of and sympathetic toward real or imaginary problems of the seller than the seller himself. This case, of course, is an argument for rotating buyers and not allowing them to assume too personal or too close a relationship with any one seller. Rotation to avoid continuous close contact does not imply that a buyer is making under-the-table deals or that there is anything ethically wrong in the relationship. It is just that occasionally familiarity breeds not contempt, but a friendship that prevents the buyer from doing the most effective job at the negotiation table. The seller, of course, should attempt to analyze the buyer's basic attitudes and conduct himself accordingly. Many firms maintain a dossier on the buyers with whom they do business.

The seller should analyze the entire history of the firm's dealings in the item or like items under consideration. Previous successes or failures in procurements with the same agency or buyer should be reviewed, and the reasons for the success or failure determined. Often precedent is a deciding factor. The seller who has developed a favorable precedent in previous procurements, and who is dealing with an acquiescent buyer willing to let precedent take the place of negotiating ability, is in a fortunate position. On the other hand, the seller who has been trapped by harmful precedents has a difficult job in justifying their change.

The first step in establishing the seller's negotiation plan is to determine precisely the objectives of the negotiation. An objective of securing exactly what is requested in the proposal is unrealistic unless the seller is certain that he is a sole source or has offered the lowest price. The latter is normally impossible to determine in negotiation.

Each element of the negotiation should be reviewed and alternative positions established, for use if necessary. Areas that have been reviewed by auditors or price analysts should be carefully studied to insure that, if there are any problems, the negotiation team is aware of them and prepared with arguments to substantiate their position.

At this stage, the seller's preparation must be of a general nature. His initial position is established in his proposal, and he cannot do too much until he gets into the negotiation and is able to secure information on the buyer's objectives.

Sellers should plan to make an opening statement that will outline their proposal in brief but complete form. Many buyers either do not have the time or do not bother to read the seller's proposal; therefore, the seller should not assume that they have. He should use a carefully prepared opening statement that provides the buyer with a complete understanding of the proposal. In preparing his opening statement, the seller should outline the main points for development.

The seller must also decide *how* to present his statement. In minor negotiations, the opening statement can be presented at the table. In major negotiations, there should be a provision for the opening statement in the agenda of the negotiation, and the statement should be presented by the seller in a formal manner, as he stands at the front of the room.

The seller should make maximum use of visual aids to clarify his position. Any negotiations can be made more effective this way. Many negotiations concerned with complex subjects need visual explanations. The simplest visual aid is the blackboard. One or more should be available in the negotiation room, and the seller should be prepared to outline his principal points on it. Charts and flow charts should be prepared in advance. Handouts should be available to guarantee that the entire audience fully understands the information presented by the seller. If possible, prototypes, models, or samples of the item under discussion should be exhibited. If the item is new, similar previous items should be displayed. Where available, television tapes, movies, slides, and simple film strips should be used to clarify the matter under negotiation.

The negotiator should have available experts in the specific areas that he anticipates will be discussed during negotiation. These may include personnel from engineering, pricing, accounting, inspection, program management, and so on. In some cases, these specialists will be on the permanent negotiation team. In other instances, they are called in only to discuss specific areas. Regardless of their permanent or temporary status, their activities should be restricted to providing expert testimony.

The seller should prepare examples of similar situations in which the seller's position has been upheld. These examples may involve the experience of the seller or even a competitor. Where the negotiation involves interpretation of the contract, decisions of the various Appeal Boards and the courts should be used to bolster the seller's arguments.

Although the seller cannot make firm plans until he gets some indication of the buyer's strategy and tactics (after all, the buyer may simply call him in and award him the contract without discussion), he should make tentative plans about how he will move from one point to another. He should find appropriate questions to identify the buyer's strategy and tactics. He should develop a tentative agenda and plan the timing of the negotiation to be sure that the objectives can be accomplished in the time available.

Next, the seller should conduct a practice session. Someone uninvolved in the negotiation should assume the role of devil's advocate and review the proposal. The advocate serves to develop the buyer's case and to try to anticipate all the alternatives available to the buyer. A practice session serves two purposes. It forces the seller to consider his proposal from the buyer's point of view, and it provides the seller's team with training in negotiation. Mistakes made in practice sessions can be corrected. Mistakes made at the table may cost substantial sums of money.

At the conclusion of his preparations, the principal negotiator for the seller should prepare a complete, written negotiation plan and present it to the management for approval. This serves two purposes. It keeps the management informed and, at the same time, commits them to supporting the negotiator's position. Negotiators are necessarily influenced by the attitudes and specific instructions of their management; however, experienced negotiators attempt to maintain as broad a position with their management as they can. They do not take extreme positions or promise too much. Management must be conditioned to expect a compromise. If they are not conditioned, the senior managers may lock themselves into adamant positions. This will affect the negotiator's ability to compromise to reach agreement. The negotiator is in the middle. He must not only convince the opposing party of the rightness of his position, but he must also justify the concessions that he makes to management. It is important, therefore, that the negotiator always keep the management completely informed about the strategy and tactics that he intends to pursue in the negotiation.

8

Planning (Buyer)

Much of the buyer's planning runs parallel to that of the seller. The principal elements of his bargaining strength are the amount of competition present, the adequacy of the cost or price analysis, and the extent of his preparation for negotiation. The buyer must cope with one more complication: he may face a tight delivery schedule that not only complicates the selection of a contractor but also seriously weakens the buyer's negotiating position. Just as the principal negotiator on the seller's team must be familiar with the product and the production processes involved, so must the buyer. It is not necessary that he understand all the technical ramifications of the item being procured, but it is necessary that he understand something of the item and the production processes involved, and their effect on cost.

In the majority of cases, the buyer is supported by technical, financial, and legal personnel, who supply information as to amount and costs of labor and material, projected overhead, and G&A rates. The buyer analyzes the information supplied to pick out areas for negotiation in which inconsistencies are present. He analyzes the seller and the members of the seller's negotiation team. He particularly reviews past experience with the seller's personnel, in an attempt to develop any patterns of behavior that may affect the negotiation. He examines the record of past negotiations to determine troublesome issues that have arisen and the methods of resolving them. He considers any particular prejudices the contractor may have in favor of certain types of contract to see if he can perhaps turn them to his advantage. He examines the record for evidences of weakness or of rapid changing of position during previous negotiations, since this is an indication of a poorly prepared proposal, or a poorly prepared seller's negotiation team. The buyer also examines the individual strengths or weaknesses of the seller's negotiation team, and attempts to determine the probable approach that the seller will take. In other words, he studies the seller's negotiation team in the same way that a horse player analyzes the past performance of animals on which he intends to bet or a pitcher studies an opposing batter.

The most important prerequisite to effective neogitation is thorough preparation. No amount of experience, skill, or persuasion on the part of the buyer can compensate for lack of preparation. This is true for one very obvious reason. Every prospective seller starts with the inherent advantage of knowing more about his proposal than the buyer does. He knows the assumptions underlying his cost estimate, the areas where contingencies have been included, and, most important, the actual cost or price level at which he will be willing to accept the contract. One of the most important tasks of the buyer is to minimize the seller's initial advantage. If the buyer enters negotiation without first having decided on the terms that will produce the best overall arrangement, and without having performed a sufficiently thorough price-cost-value analysis of the seller's offer to uncover error or potential disagreement, he will be forced to proceed on guesswork, and the seller will maintain his advantage.

Preparation for negotiation involves several major steps:

1. Gathering the facts
2. Analyzing both the facts and the many intangibles that will effect subsequent negotiations
3. Establishing the negotiation objectives on the basis of this analysis
4. Planning the strategy and tactics necessary to achieve these objectives at the negotiation table.

Perhaps the greatest obstacle to thorough preparation for negotiation by the buyer is lack of time. In many cases, buyers handle a large number of procurement actions simultaneously, so they have a limited time in which to make their analysis and develop their plans. The seller, by contrast, usually is represented by personnel who have lived with the development and presentation of the particular proposal. Time pressures alone, however, are not a valid justification for inadequate preparation. Some action can always be taken to overcome or at least minimize them. If urgent delivery dates and irreducible production lead time necessitate contract action before the buyer can adequately prepare for negotiation, a letter contract may offer a partial solution, particularly in the case of sole source procurements. If heavy work loads reduce the amount of time that the buyer can devote to preparation for any single procurement, he must exercise careful judgment in selecting the procurements that he will emphasize, and the areas within each such procurement to which he will devote major attention. Equally important, he must make maximum use of the technical, financial, and legal personnel who are available to help him.

Perhaps the most important thing that the buyer must do during the fact-finding and analysis that precedes negotiations is gain a clear and comprehensive understanding of what he is buying. This requirement is the foundation of all procurement action, and it vitally effects most steps in the procurement process. To a greater or lesser degree, the nature of the requirement controls price, contract type, contract terms, and bargaining position. If the seller's price proposal includes an estimate of engineering hours for a particular engineering task, the negotiator must understand the requirement well enough not only to evaluate the proposed level of effort but also to determine whether or not the engineering task is necessary at all. If the work to be performed is intangible in nature, has never been done before, or requires substantial technical, engineering, or production effort, the buyer must be able to determine whether an incentive contract is more appropriate than a firm fixed-price contract in spite of the apparent reasonableness of the seller's cost proposal.

Considerations of price and contract type are interrelated. The same factors that argue for use of other than the fixed-price contract cast doubt on the seller's ability to estimate his costs accurately. Conversely, in a situation that warrants a fixed-price contract but where the seller's price quotation is considered high and cannot be reduced, an incentive contract may be necessary to protect the buyer's interest. The nature of the requirements will also condition many of the terms of the contract, such as:

1. Deliveries
2. Reporting requirements
3. Warranties
4. The need for overtime
5. Patent and technical data rights
6. Kinds and amount of property to be furnished the seller.

Finally, considerations of whether the required supplies or any parts thereof have been manufactured previously, and, if they have not, whether they could be produced by other sources in time to meet the buyer's current delivery requirements, directly affect the degree of competition that exists, or is theoretically possible, and hence the relative bargaining positions of the two parties.

The better the buyer understands the supplies or services he must purchase and their intended use, the better job he can do throughout the entire contracting process, especially at the negotiation table. Such an understanding involves, but is not limited to, the following considerations:

1. The existence and nature of any plans, drawings, and specifications for the item

2. Whether the same or similar items or any parts thereof have been previously fabricated and, if so, their procurement history
3. The fabrication process
4. Any aspects of the work that either can or must be performed by other than the prime contractor
5. Engineering problems that must be met by the seller
6. The probable levels of engineering talent required to overcome such problems
7. The property that may or must be provided to the seller.

Once the negotiator fully understands what he is buying, his next step in preparing for negotiations is to analyze the price or cost estimates offered by the prospective seller. Without this analysis, the buyer cannot decide whether a seller's quotation or proposal represents the lowest reasonable price for the contract. If it does not, he needs the analysis to determine the weaknesses in the proposal that he should concentrate on during negotiations. Without adequate preparatory analysis, price negotiation may become a haggling process in which the buyer attempts to drive the price down without regard to its reasonableness or the risk involved for the seller. In time, this haggling can prove both ineffective and dangerous. If the seller begins to feel that the buyer is interested only in reducing prices and has no way of deciding what is reasonable and what is not, the seller will probably counter by quoting excessively high prices at first and then reducing them during negotiations. Reductions from an estimate that is too high to start with are not true reductions, and this reduced price will bear little relationship to the appropriate price for the job.

Some form of price or cost analysis should be made in connection with every negotiated procurement action. The method and degree of analysis, however, depend on the facts surrounding the particular procurement and the pricing situation.

Price analysis is the process of examining and evaluating a price without evaluating the separate cost elements and proposed profit of the prospective supplier whose price is being evaluated. Price analysis may be accomplished in various ways, including the following:

1. Comparison of the price quotations submitted.

2. Comparison of prior quotations and contract prices with current quotations for the same or similar end items. To provide a suitable basis for comparison, appropriate allowances must be made for differences in factors such as specifications, quantities ordered, time for delivery, buyer-furnished materials, and experienced trends of improvement in production efficiency. However, such comparisons

may not detect an unreasonable current quotation unless the reasonableness of the prior prices is established and unless changes in the general level of business and prices have been considered.

3. Use of rough yardsticks (such as dollars per pound, per unit power, or other measures) to point up apparent gross inconsistencies that should be subjected to greater pricing inquiries. Prices listed in published market prices of commodities and similar indices may be compared, together with discount or rebate arrangements.

4. Comparison of proposed prices with estimates of cost independently developed by personnel within the purchasing activity.

Cost analysis is the review and evaluation of a seller's cost or pricing data and the judgmental factors applied in projecting from known data (if any) to the estimated costs. It is carried out to form an opinion on the degree to which the seller's proposed costs represent what performance of the contract *should* cost, assuming reasonable economy and efficiency. It includes the appropriate verification of cost data, the evaluation of specific elements of cost, and the projection of these costs to determine the effect on prices of factors such as:

1. The necessity for certain costs
2. The reasonableness of amounts estimated for the necessary costs
3. Allowances for contingencies
4. The basis used for allocation of overhead costs
5. The appropriateness of allocations of particular overhead costs to the proposed contract.

Certain evaluations should be made when the necessary data are available, including comparisons of a contractor's or bidder's current estimated costs with:

1. Actual costs previously incurred by the contractor or bidder
2. Last prior cost estimate by the contractor for the same or similar item or series of prior estimates
3. Current cost estimates from other possible sources
4. Prior estimates or historical costs of other contractors manufacturing the same or similar item.

Forecasting future trends in costs from historical cost experience has primary importance. In periods of either rising or declining costs, an adequate cost analysis must include some evaluation of the trends. In cases involving production of recently developed complex equipment, even in periods of relative price stability, the buyer should undertake a trend analysis (improvement curve) of basic labor and material costs.

For detailed information on pricing, estimating, cost and price analysis, and improvement curves, the reader is referred to Sections C, D and Appendix I, *Armed Services Procurement Regulation Manual for Contract Pricing, Volume I.* Readers should review specifically the "Checklist for Cost Analysis and Negotiation," Appendix I of Chapter D-1.

In planning negotiation objectives, the buyer's first step is to analyze the seller's proposal and the cost and price analysis and technical evaluation that have been made. If any questionable areas show up, the buyer has a choice of sending his own personnel to perform additional cost and price analysis or of asking the seller for the additional cost information. When requesting cost information in the Request For Proposal, the buyer should anticipate his requirements and attempt to secure cost information in sufficient detail so that he can determine if the contractor's estimates are realistic. The 633 Form does not give sufficient cost information for proper analysis, so it should generally be backed up with detailed cost breakdowns of the various phases of the procurement. The buyer should also analyze all data available to him, such as inhouse estimates and comparative price and cost data from sellers making similar items or furnishing similar services.

Prior to the negotiation, the buyer should establish his negotiation objectives. Setting out simply to negotiate a certain percentage of the seller's estimate, or with an announced objective of negotiating the best possible price is not sufficient. The buyer should develop a dollar amount for cost and for profit or fee that he will attempt to negotiate. It is important at this stage that the buyer select alternatives, especially if the negotiation involves different sets of conditions. It should be recognized that the objectives are selected on the best available information and must be flexible. The buyer keeps his objectives from the seller, so there is no problem later if the buyer changes his objectives, either in the prenegotiation conference or in the course of the negotiation itself. Because the seller is unaware of the change, it cannot indicate weakness.

The buyer's objective is to establish a reasonable price or cost estimate for the procurement. He must be careful not to consider the seller's proposed price or cost estimate as the point from which to negotiate a reasonable price or cost, as favorable cost factors applicable to a particular contractor may result in an average cost that is a completely unreasonable price for the procurement involved.

Theoretically, the buyer's objective should be based on the point that the seller's chances of overrunning his estimate are substantially the same as the chances that he will underrun; however, this is impossible to determine in advance. The price established on a fixed-price contract should not be based on the maximum anticipated cost of performance, as this means that the seller can secure the dollar profit in his price with no effort, and will need very little effort to make a substantial increase in his profit. Nor is there any justification for allowing an unreasonably high estimate for cost-type contracts; the buyer must anticipate that the seller will budget for expenditure whatever estimated costs are provided in the contract, so that the work performed under the contract will probably expand to meet the money available to pay for it. A low price or a tight cost estimate will not necessarily harm the seller, for he has the option of increasing his efficiency.

The buyer will generally have to plan to use alternative types of contracts particularly when negotiating a fixed-price contract. This is notably important when the buyer deals with a seller for the first time. It is also significant when there are strong indications that a reasonable price will not be reached during the course of the negotiation, so that a switch to an incentive or redetermination contract will be necessary. Alternative positions also allow the buyer to move to adjust his position rapidly to meet unexpected developments during the negotiation. It is important, however, that the alternative positions be prepared to support the firm objective rather than to substitute for it.

In addition to the objective, the buyer must plan his minimum and maximum positions. The minimum position should be carefully prepared even though the buyer does not anticipate settling for it. As the buyer does not expect to use the minimum position as the basis for the settlement of the contract, he may feel that no time need be spent on its development and that he need only pick a minimum position low enough to give the buyer sufficient negotiation room. This approach ignores the fact that, if presented with a counter-offer which he considers too low, the seller may place the buyer on the defensive by asking him to justify it. If it becomes evident in the early stages of the negotiation that the buyer is presenting counter-proposals that are just for bargaining purposes and are not intelligently conceived, the buyer will lose status that may be difficult for him to recover. Consequently, the minimum position that the buyer selects should be based on a factual analysis of the cost that may result under the most optimistic forecast possible.

Even though the buyer has a lower objective, he must also choose a maximum position. In some cases, this maximum position is determined by the amount of money that is allocated to the particular procurement involved. This is not the most efficient way of determining the maximum objective. After due consideration of the seller's proposal and the cost analysis and other information associated with it, the buyer should choose the maximum on the basis of the highest costs that could be generated by the procurement. This maximum position is important because it establishes the upper limit of the buyer's negotiation range, becoming, in effect, a take-it-or-leave-it figure. Of course, this amount must be modified by the particular conditions of the procurement and an objective analysis of the buyer's bargaining position. The urgency of the requirement, the necessity for the delivery schedule, and the availability of alternate sources all have a bearing on the maximum amount that the buyer may establish. In deciding on his basic strategy and tactics, the buyer should not establish his negotiation positions on a total price or total cost, but should establish an objective and a minimum and maximum for each price or cost element. The buyer should prepare a list of his objectives and minimum and maximum positions according to Figures 8–1 and 8–2.

Next, the buyer should attempt to analyze the seller's objective and the minimum amount the seller may be expected to take for the particular contract. The buyer already knows the seller's maximum position, that has been announced in the proposal. At this stage, of course, the buyer does not know what the conditions in the negotiation will be. Perhaps the seller will come in and stand firm on his original price or cost estimate, in which case the negotiation will not be a settlement by reason and logic but will be based primarily on the exercise of bargaining strength of both parties. When negotiation is contemplated, however, the buyer should attempt to develop a reasonable estimate of the seller's possible objective and minimum position. This information can be used as a gauge in the prenegotiation conference, to feel out the seller's true position. The position of the two parties, from the buyer's standpoint, could be outlined as shown in Figure 8–3.

Very rarely do the objectives of the buyer and the seller coincide. Usually the buyer's objectives and minimum and maximum positions are considerably lower than the seller's. The difficulties that arise in the negotiation depend to a great extent on how close the objectives are and how skillful each side is in identifying the other's objective.

In planning his negotiation approach, the buyer must determine the points of difference between the seller's proposal and the buyer's objectives. There will be no objection to some parts of the proposal. The areas on which both sides agree can be handled as facts, and no further discussion of them may be necessary at the negotiation.

Assuming, however, that the seller will take the most pessimistic view of costs in the procurement and that the buyer will tend toward a more optimistic view, there will probably be a great deal of disagreement over the seller's proposal. In order to consider these areas

	Positions		
	Objective	*Minimum*	*Maximum*
Direct labor hours			
Labor rate			
Direct material amounts			
Material costs per unit			

Figure 8–1. Minimum-Maximum Objectives List Type A

	Positions		
	Objective	*Minimum*	*Maximum*
Direct engineering hours			
Engineering hourly rates			
Tooling costs			
Facility costs			
Data costs			
Manufacturing overhead			
Engineering overhead			
General and administrative			
Total Cost	XXX	XXX	XXX
Profit or Fee			
Total Price	XXX	XXX	XXX

Figure 8–2. Minimum-Maximum Objectives List Type B

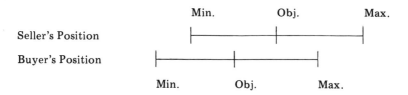

Figure 8–3. Buyer-Oriented Positions of Seller and Buyer

of disagreement most efficiently, they should be organized into issues. An issue consists of the elements upon which both sides disagree because of their opposing interests. The issues should be organized and defined as clearly as possible, as they will be the subjects of the negotiation. Clearly defining the issues is half of the battle; once the issues between the two parties are carefully delineated, then agreement or compromise becomes easier. In some cases, definition of the issues serves to point out that there are more areas of agreement than disagreement between the two parties. It is important to remember that in the preliminary stages of the negotiation, many items that one party considers as issues are not perceived that way by the other side.

The buyer should develop a tentative list of the issues involved as a result of the differences stemming from the cost and price analysis and the initial planning for the seller's proposal. The buyer should establish a position on each issue best suited to the buyer's interest and to the ultimate resolution of the entire negotiation. These issues may be set out listing the position of the buyer and the seller (see Figure 8-4).

Each issue is generally based on the individual elements of cost in the contractor's cost proposal. Generally, each issue has several ramifications. The kind, amount, and rate for direct-labor hours may be involved in one issue, and another may involve the dollar amount of overhead, the total of indirect expenses, the bases upon which the indirect expenses are allocated, and the time period covered by the projection. Issues organized in this manner provide an orderly guideline for the negotiator or buyer and give him a basis for planning his strategy and tactics; they also serve as a guide during negotiation, and can be used to summarize the progress of the negotiation as it goes along.

It is important that all issues be realistic and based on anticipated points of difference between the two parties. Recriminations by the buyer that the seller is padding his estimate are meaningless

Issue: Engineering Hours

Buyer's Position	*Seller's Position*
1600 hrs., Average rate 4.75/hr. Item includes very little design engineering. Production engineering involved not too complex and may be duplicated in overhead.	2200 hrs., Average rate 6.75/hr.

Figure 8-4. Buyer's Position on List of Issues

unless the buyer can point out exactly where he thinks the seller is padding the estimate and then counter with a more realistic estimate of his own. Issues should be as factual as possible, and devoid of emotional overtones. An emotional issue is raised only with malice aforethought, to secure an emotional reaction from the opposition.

It is important to define the issues carefully in order to identify the important ones and to take a bargaining position. A position is the stand either party takes on an issue or series of issues. Once the issues have been defined and the buyer has determined his position, he is able to make decisions about the tactics he will use in the negotiation. Remember that at this time the buyer, in planning a negotiation, is settling on a basic approach that will be modified during the fact-finding session prior to the start of actual negotiations.

The objective of the buyer under negotiated procurement is to effect a contractual agreement that is most advantageous, with due consideration to price, quality, and other factors. In essence, every action in the procurement process, from the initial development of the requirement through compilation of the list of sources for solicitation, preparation of the solicitation package, receipt and evaluation of offers received, until the contract ultimately awarded has been administered and completed, is aimed at the single objective of insuring the overall best arrangement. Unfortunately, this overall objective is frequently forgotten during the negotiation process. Too often, the main concern of negotiation is price alone or a balance of price and the most advantageous contract type. Admittedly, in many cases the latter combination will result in the best overall agreement for the buyer. But in many cases, it will not. Factors such as delivery, quality, the competence of the seller, the effect of the procurement on future competition, and so on, may far outweigh considerations of price and type of contract.

The following factors are listed as a guide for the purchasing personnel and their negotiators in the evaluation of proposals:

1. Comparison of prices quoted and consideration of other prices for similar supplies or services, with due regard to production costs, including extra pay shift, multi-shift and overtime costs and any other factors relating to price
2. Comparison of the business reputations, capabilities, and responsibilities of the suppliers who submit quotations
3. The quality of the supplies or services offered or of the same or similar supplies or services, previously furnished, with due regard to the satisfaction of technical requirements
4. Consideration of delivery requirements
5. Discriminating use of price and cost analysis
6. Investigation of price aspects of any important subcontract

7. Individual bargaining by mail or by conference
8. The nature and extent of the prospective contractor's cost reduction program
9. Effective utilization in general of the most desirable type of contract, and in particular of contract provisions relating to price redetermination
10. The size of the business concern
11. Consideration of whether the prospective supplier is a Planned Emergency Producer under the Industrial Readiness Planning Program
12. Consideration of whether the prospective supplier requires expansion or conversion of plant facilities
13. Consideration of whether the prospective supplier is located in a surplus- or scarce-labor area
14. Consideration of whether a prospective supplier will have an adequate supply of qualified labor
15. The soundness of prospective contractors' management of labor resources, including wage rates, number of workers, and total estimated labor hours, with special attention to possible uneconomical practices found in labor-management agreements or in company policy, notably in the selection of contractors for development and production of major weapons systems and subsystems
16. The extent of subcontracting
17. The existing or potential work load of the prospective supplier
18. Consideration of broadening the industrial base by the development of additional suppliers
19. The commercial production and research property that the seller will require the buyer to provide, and the elimination of the competitive advantage that might otherwise result from not having the knowledge to develop costs to provide commercial production and research property
20. Contract performance and facilities located in dispersed sites
21. Advantages or disadvantages to the buyer that might result from making multiple awards
22. The rules for avoidance of organizational conflicts of interest.

There are only two methods of pricing a product; one is by competition, the other by negotiation. In private economy, in advertised procurement, and in competitively priced negotiated procurement, the price results from the interaction of complex forces, primarily supply and demand. When these forces are not present, negotiation must take their place.

The pricing objective of the seller is easy to state. He wants to get the contract for as much money as he can. The pricing objective of the government buyer is, and should be, just a little bit different. The buyer's pricing policy must consider other objectives besides getting the contract for the lowest possible price. The regulations state that the pricing objective toward which negotiation is aimed is the price that is fair and reasonable to the contractor and the buyer.

Because of the nature of much government procurement and the differences between the objectives of various competing contractors, the term "fair and reasonable" is extremely difficult, if not impossible, to define. It may be the price that will provide a competent contractor with a reasonable remuneration for the effective application of his technical, financial, and production resources to the timely delivery of the specified items or services. More simply, a fair and reasonable price is one that provides the contractor with an incentive to do a good job and does not impair his ability to perform. This does not mean, of course, that a fair and reasonable price is always merely a product of the contractor's cost to perform. How much something costs a specific contractor is neither so little nor so much as the buyer should pay for it. In selecting a price for a particular contract, the contractor must take into account concepts of demand, competition, cost, and profit. After analysis of these factors and the other nonmonetary advantages that he will receive from the procurement, the contractor may find his price equal to, less than, or more than his accounting costs. Under those circumstances, a price that is less than his cost may still be defined as reasonable. On the other hand, the contractor's efficiency, investment in facilities, or other competitive advantage may entitle him to something more than his estimated costs plus a normal rate of profit from the buyer's standpoint.

Under a formally advertised procurement for standard commercial items, or when the buyer purchases a competitively priced or catalog item, a fair and reasonable price may be considered the "competitive market price" for the item—the lowest price for which the items can be obtained on the open market. This assumes that the competitive pressures exerted by sellers in a free and open market produce reasonable prices. As a rule, however, the competitive pressures and conditions characteristic of an open market cannot exist under a negotiated procurement. It may be impossible for potential contractors to estimate the cost of the required items or services competitively or precisely, because of the intangible nature of the items or services or because of the lack of firm plans and specifications for their manufacture. Sometimes, only a limited number of firms can perform the work. Factors in addition to price such as quality, delivery, standardization, and interchangeability of parts may have to be considered in placing the contract. The establishment of a fair and reasonable price under a negotiated procurement is a function of price or cost analysis, not of competitive pressures in the open market. Once it is determined, achieving of this price becomes a negotiation function.

Unfortunately, adoption of a general criterion, such as a "fair and reasonable price," as the pricing objective of negotiation has a major drawback; it is difficult in any particular case to draw the line between what is and what is not fair and reasonable. This problem is particularly acute when one considers the indefinite nature of much negotiated procurement, the variation in contractor capabilities, and the large part played by subjective judgment and cost estimating and analysis.

In practice, most negotiators enter into negotiations not with a single price but with a price range they consider fair and reasonable. Though this system has merit, it is not a good idea to consider the entire price range as the buyer's pricing objective, since in the long run this would undoubtedly result in a higher price. The buyer's pricing objective should generally be the lowest reasonable price, the figure at the bottom of the price range that the buyer considers to be fair and reasonable. In effect, then, the lowest reasonable price is the lowest price that provides a competent contractor with reasonable remuneration for his efforts and an incentive to do a good job. By adopting this figure rather than the vague term "fair and reasonable price" or the entire price range, as their objective, buyers and negotiators may minimize, although not eliminate, the difficulties inherent in determining a fair price.

A second aspect of the buyer's overall negotiation objective is determining the specific type of contract and terms that the buyer feels will be equitable, for both himself and the contractor. This determination is of vital importance, as the specific contract form and terms not only set forth the obligations and responsibilities of both the seller and the buyer, but also provide the framework within which all procurement action must take place. Contract types used by buyer range from the firm fixed-price type of contract under which the contractor must perform the work regardless of the ultimate cost, to the cost-plus-fixed-fee type contract under which the contractor is reimbursed for his allowable costs and paid a fee based on his initial cost estimate regardless of how he performs. Between these two extremes lie a number of flexible contract types, such as redetermination which provide for resetting of price at a later time or incentive contracts which are based on a cost-sharing formula established at the outset, usually combined with some pre-established limitations. No one of these types will fit all procurement situations. Each has its advantages and limitations that must be weighed against the circumstances of the particular procurement.

Generally, the factors governing selection of the most desirable type of contract for a given procurement include:

1. The nature and complexity of item or services required
2. The urgency of the requirement
3. The period of contract performance and the buyer's quantitative requirements under the procurement
4. The degree of competition present in the solicitation
5. The difficulty of estimating accurately the contractor's cost of performance
6. The availability of comparative data with which to evaluate the successful contractor's offer
7. The buyer's prior experience with the contractor
8. The extent and nature of the subcontracting contemplated by the contractor
9. The degree of risk involved for the contractor
10. The nature of the contractor's accounting system
11. The administrative cost to both parties generated by various contract types
12. The buyer's and seller's preference or dislike for specific types of contracts
13. The buyer's need for information on the contractor's actual cost of performance for use in pricing out follow-on procurements.

Selection of an appropriate contract type and negotiation of prices are related and should be considered together. In general, the buyer's objective should be to enter into a contract that will "place the maximum risk of performance on the seller, consistent of course with the lowest reasonable price criteria discussed above, and . . . provide the seller with the greatest incentive for efficient and economical performance." The seller's objective should be to secure a contract that involves a minimum risk to himself and the greatest profit potential.

From the buyer's standpoint, the firm fixed-price contract is the preferred type; because the price is fixed, the contract places the entire responsibility for performance on the seller. Further, because the seller keeps any cost savings he generates, theoretically the contract provides him with a maximum incentive for efficiency.

If, however, the requirement is such that the seller's cost to perform cannot be estimated or analyzed with reasonable accuracy, a more flexible type of contract is necessary to protect the seller against unwarranted cost risks. Flexibility also prevents the buyer from paying the seller additional profits that result from an unreasonable contract price and not from any production deficiencies and economies he has effected.

There are major objections to fixed-price contracts that should be considered by the buyer. Under a fixed-price contract, the buyer receives a minimum item strictly in accordance with the minimum interpretation of the specifications that he provides. Where the contract involves research and development, however, the buyer may not want to receive the minimum item but, within reasonable limits, may want the maximum item. This happens because the initial research and development costs may be only a fraction of the investment and operating costs, so that a comparatively small additional expenditure in the development stage may produce substantial savings in later investment and operating costs. In other cases, a contract may represent only a portion of the total work effort, and the buyer may want to participate to a degree in the technical decisions related to the item.

The terms and conditions of buyer contracts are basically standardized. Many of them are established by law, regulation, or executive order and are not subject to negotiation. Two major areas in which the negotiation may occur are patent rights and rights in technical data.

In practice, except for the patents and technical data issues, contract types and terms do not become controversial issues in most negotiations. The solicitation document often specifies the type of contract and the provisions that the buyer desires, and these provisions are accepted by prospective sellers as a condition for submitting quotations or proposals. In some negotiations, however, the contract type and its terms do become major areas of controversy. If this happens, both negotiators may have to compromise their primary objective: the buyer, of arriving at a contractual agreement that will maximize the seller's risk and incentive at the lowest reasonable price; and the seller, of securing the lowest risk contract at the highest possible price. It may be necessary for both to devise alternative combinations of prices and contract provisions in an effort to reach agreement during the actual conduct of negotiations.

In addition to his objectives of obtaining the lowest reasonable price for the work and a contractual instrument that will maximize the seller's risk of performance and provide him with an incentive for efficiency (consistent with the nature of the procurement required), the buyer needs assurance that all other factors and circumstances of the procurement will be in his organization's best interest. This should be an integral part of the buyer's overall negotiation objective, but it is all too frequently overlooked in negotiations.

The buyer may require the prospective seller to justify further details of his price proposal or cost quotations. This, in turn, should provide meaningful insights into just how well a seller has planned his performance for the procurement. Lack of planning may indicate that the seller is less qualified to perform the work than was initially thought, or it may raise doubts about the accuracy of his cost estimate or about the quality of his work. In some circumstances, the prospective seller's make-or-buy policies and procedures, his purchasing practices, his proposed operating and management staffing plan for the work, and his plans for capital expansion and improvement may be valid areas for discussion and analysis. To insure that he receives complete information for his negotiation, the buyer should ordinarily require submission of this type of information in his Request For Proposal. If the prospective seller has written his proposal properly, all of this information will be included. On other than fixed-price contracts, a seller's make-or-buy decisions and his purchasing practices can directly effect the cost of the procurement to the buyer, as can major capital expansions or improvements conducted during the contract period.

During negotiation, the buyer comes into personal contact with a potential supplier's management representative. This gives him a unique opportunity to gather information about various aspects of the company and about the potential contractual relationship, information that cannot be described fully in, or inferred from, a written proposal. When appropriate, a buyer should explore these areas carefully, not for the purpose of interfering with or usurping management prerogatives, but to make certain that the negotiated agreement is in fact the most advantageous one possible.

Like the buyer, a prospective seller enters the negotiation with the basic objective of arriving at an agreement that will be most advantageous to him in terms of price, contract type and terms, and other factors. It is this difference between objectives that forms the framework of the negotiation. Every prospective seller starts with the inherent advantage of knowing more about his own proposals than the buyer does. He knows the assumptions underlying his cost estimate, the areas where contingencies have been included, and above all, the actual cost or price level at which he is willing to accept the contract.

Through judicious use of technical personnel, auditors, and price analysts, the buyer must attempt to uncover as much information as possible and thus to minimize the seller's initial advantage. In preparing for the negotiations, the buyer must attempt to anticipate what the seller's specific objectives will be. When negotiation starts, he must try to identify the objectives that the seller considers most important.

Both sides must recognize that objectives of major significance to one side will frequently have far less importance to the other. If the negotiator on either side can discover the other's most important objectives, he can use them to achieve negotiation leverage, thus winning concessions in areas of major concern to him. Even when this is not the case, both sides must compare specific objectives to generate effective negotiation. The comparison identifies major issues of potential disagreement, highlighting the areas in which the negotiators must concentrate during the negotiation.

After he has completed his negotiation plan, the buyer should call a meeting of the technical, financial, and legal team members who will support him in the negotiation. He may also include personnel from other departments who may be called in to assist in specific portions of the negotiation. The primary purpose of this meeting is to establish final negotiation objectives and to develop the strategy and tactics for the negotiation.

Each team member must be acquainted with the buyer's overall approach to the negotiation, but the buyer should stress that each member should limit his participation in the actual negotiation to his own area, following the manner and extent indicated by the buyer.

Next, the buyer prepares and submits a written negotiation plan to management for their approval. The purpose of this management review is to guarantee that the buyer is properly prepared. The plan should outline the statement of work, delivery schedule, results of price and cost analysis, analysis of contract type, and the negotiation objectives and strategy. The negotiation plan should stress that the facts as presented are based on the knowledge to date, and that changes may be expected during the negotiation.

During the negotiation, if developments occur that necessitate major revisions to the pricing objectives, the buyer should call a recess, revise his plan, and resubmit it to management for approval. However, once his plan is approved, the buyer is charged with the responsibility of conducting the negotiation and must either settle the price or discontinue the negotiation based on his judgment and the opinions of other members of the team.

9 Procedures

There are two basic methods for conducting negotiations: sequential and overall. In sequential negotiation, each issue is negotiated separately, and firm agreement is reached on one before moving to another. In overall negotiation, each issue is negotiated separately, but no final conclusion is reached on any one, except as part of the final package.

Sequential negotiation involves many difficulties. It is necessary to reach agreement on the order in which the negotiation will take place. If the parties fail to agree on this, the negotiation will break down immediately. Another problem with this approach is that when the negotiators reach an impasse on an individual issue, there is no means for trading off concessions on one element of the negotiation for concessions on another.

Negotiation does not require that an agreement be reached on individual issues; rather, it involves compromises among the issues of each party. The buyer may be vitally interested in only one element of the negotiation, such as price, terms and conditions, or a combination. On the other hand, the seller's major interest may fall in an area that the buyer is quite willing to concede. Therefore, negotiation should not be conducted on the basis of reaching firm agreement on each issue but rather on the basis of discussing each area in sequence. Negotiators should reach a firm agreement if possible, but should not push for firm agreement on separate issues. Instead, they should attempt to resolve the overall issue of fairness and reasonableness in a total compromise after discussion of price, delivery, specifications, and terms and conditions. The final solution then represents not agreement on individual issues but rather a resolution of all of the points of disagreement within the agreed total contract.

The principal means of securing agreement on one issue is to make a concession on another. Because the normal negotiation involves a large number of individual elements, the agenda becomes, in effect, a road map of the negotiation and the framework within which concessions may be identified and reported. It may be assumed that in any negotiation, the parties feel more strongly on some subjects than on others. Rarely, if ever, do the positive positions of each side coincide. This may be true because the two parties cannot, in fact, make concessions on an individual issue, or because the parties simply think they cannot make concessions on individual issues. If all the issues are negotiated together, concessions made in one area become payment for concessions in another area; whereas, if each element is negotiated separately, each tends to remain an inviolate object.

Obviously, each side attempts to get the best deal possible on every element of the negotiation. At the same time, however, each side must have ready a relative order of priorities that it can use as a basis for making concessions in important areas.

It is also to the advantage of both sides for each to communicate clearly the importance it attaches to the various possible outcomes of the negotiation. This communication can be either tacit or explicit, but it must be made. By his manner of expression, his tone of voice, his facial expression, or by repeatedly stressing the issue, a sophisticated negotiator can let the other side know the relative importance that he places on each of the bargaining issues. Identifying the relative strengths of the interests of both parties is a major element of the negotiation: both negotiators should express their preferences as clearly as possible.

Another advantage of overall bargaining is that it does not require explicit agreement. Tacit agreements, which are not expressed or disclosed openly but are implied instead, are usually easier to achieve than explicit agreements. In tacit negotiation, the adversaries watch and interpret each other's behavior, each aware that his own actions are being interpreted and anticipated, and each acting with the knowledge that his actions create certain expectations.

Tacit negotiation means that the parties do not have to go through the involved and time-consuming process of agreeing on minor details necessary to achieve explicit agreement. In a tacit agreement, neither party makes a formal commitment, yet the terms of reference of a tacit agreement are quite clear to them and to others.

When a tacit agreement is reached, each side realizes that it can break the agreement without incurring a charge that it has lax negotiation ethics. This knowledge makes it easier to achieve agreement in the first place. For example, one party may say, "Well, I see your point; let's move to the next issue." Inherent in this statement is tacit agreement with the other party's position, but each party recognizes that the tacit agreement is binding only in the context of the entire negotiation. If the seller has been holding out for an overhead rate of 190% and the buyer has been offering 180%, the seller can tacitly concede the buyer's point without necessarily agreeing with the buyer's specific arguments. So, the buyer's overhead projections cannot be used as a precedent against the seller in future negotiations. Normally during negotiation, the bargaining is both tacit and explicit; even the seemingly explicit portions of the negotiation may incorporate tacit elements, and a tacit agreement may include explicit elements.

One of the advantages of piecemeal negotiation is that the process gives the parties an opportunity to cultivate confidence in each other. If the parties have never negotiated before, it may be worth their while to set up an agenda with the least important items first. If a number of tacit agreements can be reached about the minor items, then each party may be willing to make minor concessions in the hopes of developing mutual trust. In effect, this procedure allows the parties to practice their negotiation on the minor issues before they reach the more difficult major ones. At the same time, each can acquire an understanding of the other's attitudes and become familiar with his negotiation tactics and techniques. If problems do occur, they will occur in areas of minor importance to either side, and the sides can compromise quickly. Furthermore, each party learns the things it may and may not do if it intends to reach an agreement. By breaking the negotiation into small parts, each side in the negotiation can determine the good faith of the other for a relatively small price in concessions. Still further, each side can keep the other under control by insuring that the negotiation moves forward one step at a time, secure in the knowledge that it is not bound by any of the initial agreements until final agreement is reached on the entire subject of the negotiation.

This type of bargaining has another advantage. Negotiation implies some compromise of positions, which obviously entails concession by at least one side. However, negotiators are often afraid to make concessions for fear that the other side will construe concession as a sign of weakness. When the negotiation starts out with a series of small bargains, each side demonstrating to the other that it recognizes the need for compromise and a *quid pro quo* for concessions, the resulting atmosphere leads to negotiation in good faith and to recognition that compromises and counter-offers from the other side are actions to facilitate agreement rather than concessions made from weakness.

Normally in bargaining, more for one side means less for another. This concept is based on the assumption that each party places a positive value on its position. In selling a house or a car, the idea that more for one means less for the other is accurate, because both parties have fixed values on their positions. However, in commercial contracts, the negotiators normally recognize that because of the indefinite nature of much of the work performed, each side is trying to calculate what the item should cost at some time in the future. The positions taken initially by both sides, therefore, do not represent positive values. Instead, the positions are taken for the purpose of establishing the minimum and maximum figures within which each side expects to reach agreement. Thus, when the price is finally settled, it does not necessarily represent more for one and less for the other, because there are no definitive benchmarks upon which to make this judgment. Moreover, the seller still has the opportunity of performing the job as efficiently as possible to insure that his costs for completion of the work come in at less than the agreed price.

Unions often attempt to increase their bargaining position with management by conducting a prenegotiation campaign among the membership. For example, suppose that the union negotiators expect that management will offer a top limit of $2.80 per hour, but the union feels that a goal of $3.00 per hour is feasible under threat of a strike. In prenegotiation maneuvers, the union attempts to sell the membership on the fact that the management can afford, and should pay, $3.20 per hour. This automatically establishes a position from which the union can compromise to $3.00. The management negotiators can also claim a victory when they can settle for $3.00 rather than the $3.20 requested by the union. Of course, this tactic can backfire, since if the union does too effective a job of selling its membership on the validity of the $3.20 request, the membership may reject a $3.00 compromise settlement. This risk must be accepted, as in wage negotiations the prenegotiation maneuvers are a very important part of the bargaining position of both sides. If the union does not take a strong position for the $3.20 and does not sufficiently encourage the membership to expect it, the union's bargaining position weakens.

A few years ago, a major company decided to stop this type of bargaining. It adopted a policy of announcing publicly its offer in coming wage negotiations and then refusing to budge in the negotiation itself. This concept of bargaining, if it can be called bargaining, led to a large number of costly strikes. The concept reflects a complete lack of understanding by management of the internal political structure of unions and the psychology of their members. The concept struck at the basic reason for the union's existence. If the company undertook this procedure as a bargaining device, it was a bad one. However, the procedure is an effective anti-union tactic if a company actually thinks that it is in a position to weaken the union seriously. When the union actively solicits mandates from its membership about a minimum acceptable position, or when the company makes public announcements of its position from which it cannot retreat without considerable loss of face, these actions may strengthen the bargaining position of the active side, but they make securing an agreement extremely difficult, if not impossible.

Statutes, Executive Orders, and regulations such as the Armed Services Procurement Regulation (ASPR) and the Federal Procurement Regulation (FPR) limit the bargaining area in government procurement. Prior to the passage of the Cost or Pricing Data Law P.L. 87-653, whether a seller gave cost or pricing data and the extent of the data provided was subject to bargaining. Congress felt that the government was at a disadvantage with many sellers because adequate cost or pricing data was not being provided. Therefore, Congress improved the bargaining position of the government by making it mandatory that the seller furnish such data and also accept penalties in the event the data was not complete and accurate. Sellers now have no alternative except to provide the cost and pricing data when it is required, and this removes the subject from the bargaining area.

There are many other areas in which negotiation has been limited by Statute, Executive Order, or Regulation. These include such important areas as patent rights, data rights, cost principles, and so on. In addition, the buyer's bargaining position often allows him to dictate specifications and delivery schedules and to prescribe management systems to be used in the performance of its contracts.

Firm commitments on positions should not be taken prior to negotiation or too early in a negotiation. Making firm commitments too soon may create a credibility gap with the other side. Note the following:

1. Not only must the commitment be made, but it must be communicated in a believable fashion to the other party
2. It is difficult to establish a commitment and even more difficult to convince the other side of its validity and strength
3. A firm take-it-or-leave-it attitude on one side can and should be met with a take-it-or-leave-it attitude on the other
4. Both sides run the risk of establishing firm positions that are beyond the concession range of the other side, so that such a tactic may lead to a breakdown in negotiation.

A take-it-or-leave-it position is justified in the early stages of negotiation only when the seller is a sole source or when the competition is so keen that the buyer is in a position of dictating the terms of contract. If a continuous relationship is involved, a take-it-or-leave-it position on one particular issue may seriously affect future relations, not only in the period of performance but also for other procurement actions.

Some companies attempt to emulate the buyer by establishing firm policies in certain bargaining areas. If the policies cover areas that are subject to bargaining, they may aid company negotiators. However, where the policies are directly opposed to policies already established by the buyer, they can cause the company to lose a great deal of business.

Rarely does a company have the bargaining position to enforce an overall company policy contrary to that of the customer. If the buyer policy is based on a Statute or Executive Order, it may be impossible for the negotiator to compromise the issue. When the policy is established by Regulation, it is a time-consuming and difficult task to secure an exception. Companies should never establish firm policies in specific areas. Negotiation positions should be based on the factors in each individual situation.

In some cases, firms establish a policy of selling their items on a competitive or a catalog price. In procurement, these terms refer to the definitions included in the cost and pricing data policies established by companies. The ability of a firm to sell its products on a firm fixed-price basis is based on its bargaining position, which is affected only slightly, if at all, by company policy. In procurement a company can establish a single-price policy only when its bargaining position permits it to do so—for example, when the company is a sole source, or when it sells to many customers and no one customer buys enough to make it worthwhile for the company to modify its single-price position. Such positions, however, should never be taken in procurement simply because the management does not "believe in negotiation" or because the management feels that it has some inherent right to "maintain secrecy regarding its costs." Such positions result in substantial loss of business and profits. Emotional responses have no place in business decision making.

Where the scope of work is indefinite, it is difficult to see how either party can commit itself to a price of, say, $97,500. Why not $96,500 or $98,500? Normally in negotiation, the range of possible costs is too continuous to determine with finality any point between possible minimum and maximum figures upon which a firm commitment should be made.

In some cases, companies must take firm positions on maintaining a single price when they engage simultaneously in many negotiations on the same item for the same type of buyer. This holds particularly true if the item is such that the customer requires a most-favored-customer clause. Under those circumstances, a firm may be justified in maintaining a single-price position, even at the risk of losing a fairly large order. After all, a reduction in price may have to be matched elsewhere, resulting in losses far in excess of those resulting from a refusal of the single order.

When a buyer and a seller have a continuous negotiation relationship, each may be reluctant to make concessions for fear of setting precedents that may affect future negotiations. This fear of setting a precedent is often used to justify taking adamant positions in government negotiation. Where terms and conditions are involved, this can be settled by negotiating a basic agreement that is then used in all contracts between the parties. If the question involves price or cost, refusing to make a concession for fear of setting a precedent is unrealistic.

The problem generally arises with such items as overhead rates, labor rates, and so forth. Since these are generally applied to direct labor and material bases, which vary with each procurement, it is difficult to see why so much importance should be attached to them. No negotiation should deadlock on such issues, because they can be resolved in an overall agreement on price without necessarily placing the negotiators in the position of agreeing to any specific element of cost.

One common method of controlling commitments in negotiation is to conduct negotiations through agents rather than principals. The principal decision maker should never engage directly in negotiation, except perhaps in its final stages to iron out a deadlocked major issue, and then only with the principal on the other side. By using agents at negotiations, both principals insulate themselves from the necessity of making immediate decisions. This provides a hierarchy of appeal to which issues that cannot be resolved at the negotiation table can be forwarded. Under these circumstances, both negotiators recognize that they are operating as agents for another, and that, of necessity, their ability to make concessions is constrained by their instructions from their principals.

In negotiation, when one side refuses to make concessions, it is common for the other side to claim that the negotiator "does not have the authority to negotiate." This problem is stressed in buyer negotiations, but it is a negotiation technique that should fool no one. It should be obvious to both sides that each is negotiating within a range of authority.

When the authority of one side to negotiate is, in fact, limited, and this condition is identified, negotiation ceases, and the process becomes simply a test of bargaining position and willpower. The tactic of limiting the negotiation authority of the actual negotiators may be acceptable under certain circumstances. The ability of the negotiator to make concessions may be an advantage under some circumstances, but certainly not in all. Under some circumstances, if one side knows that the other negotiator is powerless to make agreements on a specific issue, then any concessions made on this issue will have to be made by the party that *does* have the flexibility. When the authority of one party to a negotiation is restricted, that party is in a position to throw the blame for a breakdown in negotiations on the other side.

Some buyers may attempt to bypass the seller's representative and to negotiate with the management. This should be discouraged by insisting that the buyer's supervisor talk with the seller's supervisor, and so on up the management ladder. If the buyer insists, management should meet with him and be courteous, but should make absolutely no changes to the company's position except through established channels. If they do make any concessions, they can be sure that the same buyer will always insist on dealing with them instead of with their representative.

In some cases, the situation is reversed. Sometimes the seller is not satisfied with the deal offered by the buyer and attempts to get a better one from the buyer's management. He should also be given courteous treatment and a negative response, unless the management wishes to destroy the morale of their buyers and face the necessity of conducting all future negotiations themselves with that supplier.

Sometimes occasions arise when negotiation is not possible. Lawyers have a saying, "When the facts are on your side, quote the facts; when the law is on your side, quote the law; and when neither is on your side, yell!"

For example, in one case a seller took a subcontract that involved the development and production of a very complicated electronic item. He lost approximately three million dollars on the initial contract. The contract also contained an option for a further quantity at a specified price. The seller anticipated a further substantial loss on this option quantity, so he requested that the buyer increase the price of the option quantity. The buyer refused and exercised the option.

Legally, the seller was bound by the terms of the contract. However, the loss involved on the initial order, combined with that anticipated on the option quantity, would have seriously impaired the financial stability of the firm, and most important, probably would have resulted in the president of the firm losing his position. The seller had one major element in his favor, however. The buyer was completely dependent upon the seller for a supply of the items. If the items were not supplied, the buyer would have been unable to meet his commitments on his prime contract, in which case he would have incurred substantial incentive penalties, in excess of the amount required to bail out the seller. The subcontractor flatly refused to deliver the option quantity without an increase in price, on the basis that no firm should be asked to commit industrial suicide.

In this case, the buyer's alternatives were limited. He could default the seller and purchase the item elsewhere; however, this was impossible under the circumstances. He could sue the seller for non-performance; however, even if he ultimately won a settlement against the seller, the buyer's loss under his prime contract would have been greater than the seller's. Further, the buyer had no assurance that the subcontractor would be solvent enough in the future to pay any claim for settlement. Finally, the seller was under pressure from his customer to maintain delivery schedules. Under the circumstances, the adamant stand of the subcontractor won the day, and the prime contractor was forced to give the subcontractor an increase in price. When circumstances such as this arise and both sides have a great deal to lose, your ability to impress the other party with the fact that you are more irrational or intransigent than he is may be the only negotiation method you can use. On the other hand, if both parties are adamant, both may lose. A refusal to negotiate will result in an advantage only if the other side has more to lose.

10 Tactical and Strategical Negotiation

Strategy can been defined as Skillful management in getting the better of an adversary or attaining an end, the method of conducting operations, especially by the aid of maneuvering or stratagem. The practical adaptation of the means placed at your disposal to the attainment of the object in view. Strategy should not be based on overcoming resistance in negotiations but on effective planning to reduce the possibility of resistance.

The three principle strategic concepts are the offensive, the defensive, and the defensive-offensive.

The seller's choice is obvious. He has presented a proposal based on his best analysis of the concepts of demand, competition, and cost that are applicable to the particular procurement. He certainly has no justification for going on the offensive. On the other hand, the seller's acceptance of a completely defensive tactic means that the buyer is in a position to whittle down the approach of the seller, with no objections. The defensive-offensive strategic concept implies that the seller, having presented a proposal presumably based upon his best analysis of the situation at the time, rests on his proposal until such time as the buyer can demonstrate that the proposal is not a reasonable one. When a seller adopts a defensive-offensive strategy, the burden of any action rests upon the buyer, who will be forced to go on the offensive and attempt to convince the seller that his proposal, while meritorious, is not acceptable to the buyer.

The seller explains and defends his initial proposal against attacks by the buyer but is always looking for an opportunity to move to the offensive to blunt the strength of the buyer's attack. He may do this in a number of ways. For example, if the buyer states that the seller's price is too high, rather than taking the defensive to explain why it is not, the seller could move to the offensive and question the basis of the buyer's statement. He could state that the fact of his presence is proof that he wants to secure the contract, that he has made his best and most reasonable offer based on his knowledge of the procurement as he sees it, but that if the buyer has some information that would enable him to do it for a lesser figure, he will be happy to consider it. The seller could then suggest that both of them review in detail the elements of cost that form the basis of the buyer's lower offer. In effect, the seller moves to the offensive by negotiating the buyer's cost breakdown. This may expose the fact that the buyer has no detailed backup for his offer, in which case the seller could quickly change the topic, with the obvious inference that the buyer's position had no justification in fact and was merely a negotiation gambit. This is a particularly effective approach when a buyer makes an initial offer that is extremely low.

Another method by which the seller can go on the offensive is to let the buyer know early in the initial negotiation sessions that the seller is aware of the relative bargaining positions of the two parties, based on such criteria as sole source, delivery requirements, or failure of the buyer to make an adequate cost or price analysis.

The seller should maintain his defensive-offensive strategy during the entire negotiation. This presents the buyer with the necessity of proving that the seller's position is wrong. Recognizing this strategy, the buyer's obvious counter strategy is to attempt to place the seller in a position of proving that his proposal is correct.

Tactics can be defined as a method or procedure for gaining advantage or success. In other words, strategy deals with the planning or directing of a project while the tactics include the actual processes and maneuvers used to implement the strategy. The principles of tactics for negotiation may be summarized in the following points:

1.   Adjust your end to your means
2.   Always keep your objective in mind
3.   Use a line or course of least resistance
4.   Exploit the line of least resistance
5.   Take an approach that offers alternative objectives
6.   Insure that your plan is adaptable to changing circumstances
7.   Do not put your weight behind an approach while your opponent is on guard
8.   Do not renew an attack along the same line or in the same form after it has failed once.

In the early stages of the negotiation, the buyer's overall strategy must be an offensive one. He has a choice, however, of various tactics to use, based primarily on his method of presenting the issues. The buyer may choose to present the most important issues first, on the grounds that if the important issues can be resolved, the minor ones will generally be easy to resolve. On the other hand, he may decide to present first the issues on which he expects the most opposition, with the idea that if the more troublesome issues are out of the way, the other, perhaps more important issues can be solved more readily. Again, he may decide to present either the least important or the least contentious issues first and attempt to establish a pattern of agreement. He may use the negotiation concerning the unimportant issues to feel out the positions and objectives of the opposing parties, and to give himself an opportunity to evaluate the representatives of the seller. In other cases, he may attempt to arrange and to present the issues in an order requiring that if a concession is made on one issue, a concession will have to be made on other subsequent issues in order to be consistent. The buyer must also plan his basic offensive tactics. Generally he has three choices: reveal no position; reveal a minimum position; or reveal the minimum and the objective.

The buyer can elect not to reveal a position and attempt to move the seller from one position to another until he reaches the buyer's objective. This strategy is used quite often when the buyer has no cost or price analysis or other realistic information upon which to base his negotiation. The buyer prepares a series of questions or simply takes the seller's proposal and follows it point by point, demanding justification, trying to pick up inconsistencies in the seller's explanation, and then pursuing the inconsistencies in an attempt to convince the seller that he should move from the original position.

If the seller is alert and determines by appropriate counterquestions and redirected questions that the buyer has no sound basis for his attempt to force the seller to reduce his objective, the seller may simply answer the buyer's questions, justify his position on individual issues, and stand pat on his original proposal.

This approach is effective for the buyer only when the seller is in a weak position or anxious to secure the contract on almost any terms. It is sometimes used as an initial strategy to move the seller from an impossible position to a negotiable position. The buyer should never attempt to negotiate with the seller when the seller's proposal is obviously unrealistic. Concessions made from a position that is initially too high are not real concessions. The buyer, therefore, may follow a strategy of revealing no objectives or positions of his own and of making no counterproposals until the seller's position becomes a realistic one; then the buyer may adopt one of the following procedures for the balance of the negotiation.

The second and most commonly used strategy occurs after an initial fact-finding session, when the buyer reveals his minimum position as an initial counterproposal. The buyer's initial position or counterproposal must be a realistic one. If he makes a proposal that is obviously too low, he lays himself open to a counterattack from the seller, placing the seller in a position to demand that the buyer justify his offer. If the buyer has no realistic basis for his counter-proposal, he finds himself in the position of not bargaining in good faith, and thus loses face.

An initial counterproposal should never be offered and immediately withdrawn. In the initial stages of negotiation, the buyer has absolutely no idea of the seller's real objective, so his strategy should be to offer a realistic counterproposal and to use it to test the strength of the seller's positions. Each offer and counteroffer should be vigorously negotiated and neither side should move until the other has offered convincing evidence that the position is no longer attainable.

The initial counterproposal from the buyer establishes the range of the negotiation since, at this point, the minimum point is the buyer's counterproposal and the maximum point is the original proposal by the seller. The buyer should never make a counter-proposal until the seller's proposal is a reasonable one. Negotiations tend to move toward some middle position. If the seller gets the buyer to accept his unrealistic initial proposal as a basis for negotiation, the net result of the negotiations may end up far above the legitimate objective of the buyer.

Once a realistic range has been established for the negotiation, the individual issues have to be examined and negotiated separately. These are used as a basis for movement by both sides, in an attempt to reach an objective or a reasonable settlement of the entire contract. The timing and the size of the moves must be carefully planned. No move should be made simply to compromise. A concession should be made only when the other side has earned it by presenting convincing logical evidence that their position, if not right, is at least sounder than the position of the other party.

The third approach open to a buyer is to reveal the minimum figure and then immediately to offer his objective. This provides the buyer with very little bargaining room and may be considered a sign of weakness by the other party. A buyer who uses this strategy is basing his approach on either his ability to convince the seller of the reasonableness of the approach that he is offering, or his ability to force him to take it. This approach is a difficult one to sustain, considering all of the problems that can arise in a negotiation. It is improbable that a buyer can develop an objective representing the best possible deal that he can secure from the seller. The approach is based on the philosophy that the buyer and his team can establish a valid independent estimate. If the item is a complex one and the buyer does not have access to historical costs, the probability that the buyer can initially establish a valid cost estimate is extremely remote.

In the preliminary planning stages, the buyer may find it difficult to determine precisely which approach to use. If he is certain that the seller is anxious to secure the contract, and the bargaining strength and economic factors are on the side of the buyer, then the buyer should consider the first approach, namely, to reveal no minimum or objectives to the seller and to attempt to use the seller's eagerness to force him to contract at the buyer's price.

Where the bargaining strength of the two parties is more equally divided, the buyer would be safer in using the second approach, that is, after an initial fact-finding session, to present a minimum position as an initial counteroffer. This establishes a more realistic position and provides the buyer with a position from which he can make concessions in case the seller's bargaining position or attitude towards the negotiation turns out to be stronger than anticipated. The same thing may happen if the buyer attempts to use the first approach. He may find that he has overestimated his bargaining strength and the seller's eagerness to sell, or he may find that the seller has overestimated his bargaining strength. Then, to prevent the negotiation from bogging down, or even perhaps breaking up, the buyer must be flexible enough to change his negotiation approach and present a counterproposal to put the bargaining on a more even footing than is usual in the first approach.

The dangers in the buyer's announcing his real objective early in the negotiations have already been noted. The announcement places him in a position of standing adamantly on his first proposal. This may cause the negotiation to break down if the seller is not convinced that the buyer's announced objective is a true one and attempts to force the buyer to take a different position. Such a position on the part of the buyer presents him with the same problems that the seller faces when he attempts to stand pat on a fixed price.

11 Methods

Essentially, negotiation is communication, and the techniques of negotiation are the same as those used for communicating ideas for any purpose. The fact that the communication involves either convincing the other party that you are right or, if that is not possible, attempting to reach an agreement that will maximize the benefits to both parties, means that communication skills become more important.

Basically, negotiation involves the use of logic, persuasion, and in some cases, economic pressure to reach agreement in areas in which the opposing parties have divergent interests. There are some techniques of communication, debate, and persuasion that are more effective and more generally used than others. Some of the more important ones are discussed below.

The negotiation of a contract or subcontract may involve ten or fifteen major points of difference between the two parties and many more minor points of difference. In order to reach a final agreement, it is necessary to consider these points in an orderly fashion. Therefore, they should be considered one at a time, and both sides should be certain that the other side understands the problem being discussed.

In defining a problem, it is best to establish clearly the facts and conditions of the problem and the assumptions that each side is using in the discussion. Definitions should be clearly understood, so that the words used mean the same thing to each party. Last, the criteria that will be used to evaluate a possible solution should be developed.

Defining or stating the problem is the first requirement, but often during the negotiation, the problem becomes sidetracked or extraneous issues creep into the agenda. Then it becomes necessary to restate or redefine the problem in order to resume the negotiation in an orderly fashion. Once an issue is advanced for negotiation, both sides should confine their discussion to the issue until it is finally resolved, or until it is deliberately put aside for future consideration. Of course, either side may deliberately attempt to sidetrack or to evade a particular problem. So both sides should be on the alert to recognize evasion in the other party and to evaluate the reason for it.

Questions are the most important tool available to a negotiator. With a properly phrased question, he may attack an opponent's position, defend his own position, evade a touchy question, or control the progress and the trend of the negotiation session. Throughout the entire negotiation, the questions asked and the answers given by each side are the principal methods of resolving the problems in the negotiation.

A question must be selected and worded according to the purpose for which it is asked. Questions may be general or specific, depending on the nature of the response desired. The most effective questions are those which cannot be answered with a simple "yes" or "no": these are the who, what, when, where, why, and how questions. The manner in which the question is asked and the attitude displayed by the questioner has a strong bearing on the manner in which the question is received and answered. In negotiation, questions become very important tools, and should be carefully planned, thoughtfully selected, and skillfully used. The technique of questioning intelligently and with purpose is an art. There are many types of questions.

Overhead. This question is asked of a group of people. It can be used to introduce the issue, to establish the limitations of the discussion, and to define terms on which there may be misunderstanding. Example: "What were you thinking of in terms of special procedures in this area?"

Direct. These are addressed directly to one individual and are couched in specific terms. In negotiation, the direct question is a most effective means of taking the offensive, because it requires an answer from the person to whom it is addressed. Once a question is asked, the questioner should remain absolutely silent until the answer is given, for generally direct questions are used by the buyer in an attempt to secure an explanation from the seller. The buyer should refrain from any further conversation until he receives an answer. This places the opposite party in the position of either answering the question, evading the question, pretending to misunderstand the question, or redirecting the question. Any vagueness or refusal to answer may sometimes provide more information than the answer to the question itself. Example: "Can your company meet this delivery schedule?"

Leading. A question may be phrased so as to suggest an answer. Example: "Don't you think our price is a reasonable one?"

Factual. A question may require the person questioned to provide information. Example: "What is the base of allocation of your overhead rate?"

Require Explanation. This question requires explanation by the use of such words as "why," "when," "where," "what," "who," and "how."

Ambiguous. The question may have two or more meanings. No question should be answered in negotiation, particularly by the seller, unless the respondent understands the intent of the question, the ramifications of the question, and the effects of the answer on the particular matter under discussion. Example: a buyer may say, "These labor hours do not look right to me. Please explain them." The buyer may think the labor hours are too high, or he may think that they are too low. Because the seller cannot determine from the question the reason behind it, he should refuse to answer it until the purpose for which it was asked becomes apparent.

Redirected. While the question technique is the best offensive tool available to a negotiator, particularly the buyer, question technique can also be used as a defensive measure. The redirected question returns an ambiguous or potentially embarassing question by reversing it. In the example above in which the buyer asked the seller an ambiguous question concerning labor hours, to avoid answering this question and to force the buyer to explain why the question was asked, the seller may rephrase the question and reverse it to the questioner. Example: "Just which aspect of the labor hours interests you?" This technique may be used a number of times: at that point the buyer could reverse the question back to the seller by stating, "You know what part of the labor hours that I am interested in." Of course, this method should not be carried to ridiculous extremes. The obvious way to stop it is to ask a specific question regarding the point at issue. Regardless of how many times a question is reversed, however, no negotiator should begin to answer a question until he fully understands the meaning and intent of the question.

Relay. A relay question is a reverse question that is passed on to another person at the table. Using the same example, noted previously, where the buyer requests information from the seller regarding his labor hours, at this point the seller could rephrase the question and redirect it to a member of the buyer's team, say the production specialist or engineer who participated in the cost or price analysis. Example: "We have presented considerable information in our proposal concerning the quantity of our labor hours and the methods by which we arrived at them. Mr. Jones [the buyer's engineer] has reviewed our proposal, and I know he paid particular attention to this subject. What were his findings with regard to our labor-hour estimate?" The buyer should break into the discussion at this point and insist that all questions be directed to him and not to a team member.

Controversial. Although it is very seldom a good policy deliberately to inject controversy or argument into a negotiation, sometimes it becomes necessary or useful as a smokescreen, arousing emotional response from the other side of the table, either to sidetrack an issue, or to break down the other person's control in the hopes that he will reveal information that he would not discuss under ordinary circumstances. Example: "I don't think you really want to reach an agreement on this contract, considering the obstructionist tactics you are using. Well, do you?"

Provocative. This question is designed to incite. Example: "Are you negotiating with us or are you simply stating a position from which you do not intend to move?"

Yes or No. This calls for a "yes" or "no" answer and is one of the most dangerous questions asked in a negotiation. A question that can be answered this way should be asked only if the questioner thinks that the answer will be in the affirmative, or unless he is willing to accept a negative reply. Once a person verbalizes an objection, it becomes more difficult to get him to change his mind later, when status and face-saving become involved.

The actual wording or phrasing of each question depends upon the purpose and the exact situation at the time it is asked. The following list shows how the wording of the question ties in with its purpose and how you may indicate the kind of response you desire by your choice of phrasing. For example, the buyer may ask the seller to compare his present price with past prices for the same or similar items, or he may use a question to express strong doubt as to the validity of the seller's estimate. Just so, the seller can move from the defensive to the offensive by requesting the buyer to justify his position on particular issues. The questions should be phrased according to the purpose and requirements of the moment.

Classify. Demands the assembling, arranging, and grouping of facts according to some common characteristics

Compare. Requires the detection of resemblance and difference among facts

Criticize. Exacts good judgment and a careful analysis of the subject

Define. Necessitates the determination of definite boundaries or limits of a subject, and the fixing of a clear meaning

Describe. Calls for the selection and portrayal of the features or qualities characterizing a subject

Discuss. Compels a minute examination of a subject, presenting pro and con considerations, and adducing arguments or reasons in support of a position or attitude

Explain. Necessitates a clarification of any points that may obscure a subject, and also makes a subject clearly intelligible

Illustrate. Calls for examples that will explain or clear up the subject under consideration

Interpret. Necessitates bringing out the meaning of a subject in the light of an individual's belief or judgement

Justify. Demands showing that a thing is reasonable or warranted

Outline. Necessitates sketching or indicating the main points in a discussion, argument, or process

Review. Compels going over a subject deliberately and giving it a critical examination

Summarize. Asks for the presentation of a subject in a concise manner

Trace. Requires following in detail the development or progress of some subject

Verify. Exacts proof that a thing is true

Although the wording of questions will vary with their purpose and the stage of the negotiation, some important things should be kept continuously in mind. When seeking information, word your question clearly and leave no doubt as to your exact meaning unless you are deliberately asking an ambiguous, controversial, or provocative question. Questions that can be answered "Yes" or "No" should be avoided, particularly by the seller. Your method of phrasing a question and the tone in which you ask it can influence both the immediate response and the general attitude. For example, you can put someone on the defensive by asking him to prove his statement, to justify his position, or to defend his proposal. A question can be phrased in either commendatory or derogatory terms.

Questions should be asked in a normal conversational tone, allowing the question itself to carry the emphasis. All questions should be phrased as if the questioner is asking a legitimate question and expects an answer, whether or not he does. Once you ask a question, insist that it be answered. However, when a question remains unanswered, don't let the person flounder indefinitely. Make it obvious that you recognize his evasion or failure to answer the question.

Avoid questions that antagonize, create a feeling of inferiority, or cause other unfavorable reactions, unless you ask the question with malice aforethought and as part of the general tactics pursued at that particular time in the negotiations. This tactic is dangerous and should be used rarely, if at all.

Finally, keep personalities and sarcasm out of all questions. The question is a very fine offensive tool for both parties, and a redirected question can be used to defend against a question that you do not wish to answer, but rudeness is out of place. For example:

1. To call attention to a point that has not been considered, "Has anyone been thinking about this part of the problem?"
2. To ask how strong an argument is, "How much importance does the buyer attach to this part of the provision?"
3. To get back to causes, "Why did the price analyst take this position?"
4. To call attention to the source of information or argument, "Did the engineer have time to make a thorough analysis of our proposal?"
5. To suggest that the discussion is wandering from the point, "Just which issue on the agenda are we considering now?"
6. To suggest that all available information on the issue has been given, "Can anyone offer any information on this point in addition to what has already been given?"
7. To call attention to unsuspected difficulties or complexities in the problem, "I wonder if the problem isn't more difficult than we had at first supposed?"
8. To register steps of agreement, "Am I correct in assuming that we agree on this point?" (Be careful. This is a "Yes" or "No" question.)
9. To call attention to points of disagreement, "Are we agreed to disagree for the time being?"
10. To suggest that the majority of issues have been resolved, "Well, it looks like we can wrap this up, doesn't it?"
11. To suggest that the contract is not finally agreed to, "Shouldn't we think this matter over and reconsider it at our next meeting?"
12. To suggest that nothing will be gained by further delay, "After all, can we hope to get any more information or ideas?"

13. To suggest that each side may well come part way in arriving at a course of action, "Doesn't the best course of action lie somewhere between our two positions at this point?"

The subtle shading of meaning in different words, seemingly the same, is most obvious in international negotiations, where a simple shift from "may" to "will" can signify major changes in relations between two countries. The choice of words also has a powerful affect on negotiations. Strong words that provoke strong feelings should be avoided. So should words which imply antagonism.

The English language is very complex. It has many synonyms, each of which conveys fine nuances of meaning. The effective negotiator must have a large vocabulary with which he can express exactly the shade of meaning he intends. Consider the difference in impact of the following statements.

1. "It looks as if we are at an impasse on this issue." *Impasse* is defined as a situation from which there is no escape, a difficulty without solution.
2. "You and I are irreconcilably opposed on this issue." *Irreconcilable* is defined as that which cannot be brought into agreement.
3. "We seem to disagree on this point." *Disagree* is defined to differ in opinion, to quarrel or dispute.
4. "You and I differ on this point." *Differ* is defined as to be of opposite or different opinions.
5. "It looks like you don't know what the hell you are talking about [again]." You add the last word, of course, only if you want to rekindle all the flaming discussions that occurred before.

Other sentences that are almost guaranteed to prolong or break up a negotiation are:

"Well, I am glad that you finally grasped the problem."

"Are you sure you understand the meaning of what you are saying?"

"I am glad to see that you agree with me."

"Do you understand what I am saying?"

In reference to the last point, if the other person doesn't understand you, it may not necessarily be because he is stupid. It may be because you are not explaining yourself properly.

Is something merely "unfavorable" to you? If that is the only word you can think of, you should look up the meaning of the following words, all of which are synonyms for "unfavorable";

adverse, contrary, disadvantageous, inauspicious, inopportune, prejudicial, unfortunate, unpropitious, and ill-disposed. Moreover, you may consider the other negotiator to be your antagonist, competitor, rival, adversary, foe, enemy, or a die-hard bitter-ender.

Skill with words is absolutely essential to the successful negotiator. He must be able to choose a word that, in combination with the proper facial expression and tone of voice, will convey his exact meaning to the other side of the table. Remember, not only what you say but how you say it will strongly affect any negotiation. Don't arouse needless antagonism and trouble for yourself with sloppy language.

One of the most effective audio-visual techniques is the human face combined with the human voice. By modifying either, you can also modify, change, or expand the meaning and intent of the spoken word. Much of your impression of someone else is based on your response to his face and to his tone of voice. This is particularly true in negotiation. For example, suppose one person says to another, "You are a really nice guy." If that sentence is said with an affectionate tone of voice and a pleasing expression, it means exactly what it says. However, change the facial expression to a grimace, harshen the tone of voice, place full emphasis on the word "nice," and the sentence becomes an insult.

Everyone should learn to control his facial expression and tone of voice so that he can use them to emphasize the real meaning of the words he uses to convey his ideas. This is not important only in negotiation. It is also important in our everyday life, if we want to communicate properly with our fellow beings. The words we use, the emphasis that we place on certain words, the tones of voice that we use, and the expressions on our faces as we are speaking can all modify the meaning of our words. We can take the sting out of an otherwise harsh statement, make an insult out of a seemingly friendly statement, or provide a subtle means of letting the other person know the importance that we attach to our particular statements.

While talking, study your facial expression in a mirror. Many people have unconsciously developed a bland facial expression that gives no indication of their real feelings. There is no way for the people with whom they are communicating to develop an appreciation of what they really mean. When a bland facial expression combines with a flat monotonous voice, the unfortunate individual becomes almost impossible to listen to for any period of time.

The human voice should be treated like the musical instrument it is. It is capable of beautiful or harsh sounds; it is capable of whispering or shouting; it can express rage, fear, determination, or love.

One method of checking your tone of voice is to use an ordinary dictating machine. Although the range of these machines is not too great, it will give you some idea of the range of expression in your voice, and will give you a means of practicing the proper use of this effective negotiation tool. Dictate several letters into a dictating machine and listen carefully on the play-back to the tone and expression in your voice. Pay careful attention to idiosyncrasies or habits of speaking that could possibly annoy others. Next, read a poem into the machine and try to put as much expression into it as you can; then listen to yourself. The combination of the two should be enough to convince you of the necessity of the proper use of the voice as a communication device.

Though a negotiator is not expected to recite a soliloquy from *Hamlet*, the would-be-negotiator can learn a great deal from watching actors in movies, plays, and on television, observing the way they use facial expression and tone of voice to emphasize the meaning of words.

12 Techniques

A number of tactics and techniques have been developed for use in negotiation. The experienced negotiator should be familiar with all of them and may even find it desirable or necessary to use them all in a given situation. However, techniques must be used carefully and discriminately, especially those involving pressure, just to show expertise as a negotiator.

The best negotiation technique is the use of logic and persuasion. Economic pressure can be used, but it should be applied skillfully and should never be openly discussed. Negotiation cannot be conducted in a highly charged emotional atmosphere.

It is impossible to apply the same strategy, tactics, and techniques to each negotiation. A negotiation is affected by:

1. The nature of the issue: initial contract, change, letter contract, termination claim, cost principles, and so on
2. The differences between the two parties
3. The relative bargaining strength of the two parties
4. The personalities involved.

The more experience two negotiators have in negotiating with each other, the more difficult it will be for either to use the same techniques, particularly any that involve bluffing. Like other game players, they will become familiar with each other's playing habits, and this will reduce the number of techniques available to each.

Following are a number of techniques that are used in negotiation, either deliberately or by accident. Since the seller normally takes the defensive-offensive position, claiming that he has submitted his best offer initially and therefore sees no reason to negotiate, the buyer normally has to take the offensive. As a result, many of the techniques discussed are for the buyer. Where appropriate, the seller's possible responses to the techniques are also discussed.

One of the best negotiation techniques is to combine logic and persuasion with clear, simple language. Many disagreements arise from semantics, not real differences of opinions. To reach agreement, it is necessary that each side understand the other. To avoid misunderstandings, therefore, negotiators should:

107

1. Use short sentences
2. Use short words and those within the other side's frame of reference; use the other side's style and examples in developing your own arguments
3. Repeat important points often, using slightly different language each time.

To insure complete understanding, never use words peculiar to one discipline or technical terms without carefully defining their meaning. Normally, it is better not to use specialized terms at all, but to use other, simpler words that are certain to be within the framework of knowledge of everyone at the negotiation table.

A negotiation technique that may be used to advantage is making the other party appear unreasonable. This can be done by making concessions on minor issues and then asking in return for concessions on major issues. During negotiations, you may make numerous but relatively unimportant concessions so that when a major issue arises, you can claim in return a concession on the major issue. If the other side refuses to reciprocate, you imply that one party, yours, is being eminently reasonable and the other is not—unless, of course, it is willing to compromise on the major issue.

The buyer may place the seller on the defensive by asking a whole series of questions concerning each element of the seller's cost estimate. This is done to uncover areas in which discrepancies exist or with which the seller's representative is not familiar. The seller can counter this technique by flooding the buyer with irrelevant data. Then, if the buyer seeks further clarification on an individual issue, the seller may indicate that he has given the buyer everything he has asked for and criticize him for being unreasonable in persisting on a single issue.

Both sides can blame their reluctance to compromise on third parties. The seller can explain his reluctance to compromise or his objections to the buyer's position by stating that he is willing to compromise but it wouldn't be fair to the company's stockholders or it would be against company policy or that his management would not approve the concession of a particular point. To counter, the buyer must first determine whether or not the given statement is authentic. If it is true, he must then determine if the factor that prevents the company from compromising can and should be changed by direct approach to top management. If, on the other hand, the seller's position is exposed as mere bluff, his bargaining position is materially weakened, and the buyer's position improves considerably.

The buyer may use variations on this technique to advantage

under appropriate circumstances. He may, for example, cite procurement regulations or policies as reasons for his inability to do something. He is relatively safe in this, because the seller's representatives are rarely familiar enough with the regulations to dispute them. The buyer may argue that he does not have enough money to accept the seller's offer. This can be countered by a suggestion that the buyer should reduce the scope of the work of the contract to agree with the money he has available. The buyer can place the blame for his reluctance to compromise on higher authority, perhaps by making a statement to the effect that they would never go along with the proposal but would simply reject the whole deal, which would result in having to start all over again.

It is true that normally a buyer must secure the approval of his management, but management will usually go along with the deal recommended by the buyer, unless major problems exist. Therefore, when this last technique is used, the seller should suggest that since it is a good deal and has the buyer's approval, the buyer should process the deal through for approval with his recommendation.

Deliberate misinterpretation of a statement made from the other side of the table is a device to make that side defend its point of view or discuss the subject further. This device is particularly useful when the other negotiator's meaning is not clear. But it may backfire, because in proving that you misunderstood him and in clarifying his statement, he may simply strengthen his argument.

A technique that differs slightly from deliberate misinterpretation is pretending that you do not quite understand the statement made by the other side. This technique is appropriate when you feel that the statement is not clear or that the other negotiator's thinking lacks organization. Your pretended lack of understanding will force him to clarify both his statement and his own thinking, while you gain time to organize your position.

Pro and con analysis is a device in which a party lists the points in favor of a proposition under one heading and those against it, under another. The complete list forms a clear, concise analysis of the problem. In certain situations, it may be helpful to encourage the other side to get all the facts and consider both points of view before arriving at a conclusion. Theoretically, this technique should end up proving that the position advocated by the analyzer is the logical answer to the problem. It is particularly useful for summarizing the other side's arguments and using them to your own advantage. It can be used to correct faulty thinking, to force an impartial consideration of the problem, and to put the negotiation on a professional level. It can also be used to correct an obvious mistake or misunderstanding by the other side of the table without stating flatly that they are wrong.

The technique of agreement and rebuttal, the "yes—but" technique, is often a valuable approach to negotiations. Its use makes the negotiator seem more reasonable and conciliatory than he may really be, because he is couching his disagreement with the other side in terms of agreement. Most important, it helps the negotiator to develop arguments that use the contractor's own words and examples.

One of the best negotiation techniques may be genuine ignorance, obstinacy, or simple disbelief that the other party will carry out a threat. Someone once said, "You can negotiate with a liar, but you cannot negotiate with a fool." One effective technique to bolster a weak case is to put a half-informed person (he is more dangerous than a completely ignorant person) opposite a skilled, informed negotiator. One of the most painful things in the world is to watch a professional negotiator, accustomed to dealing with other professionals, attempt to negotiate with an uninformed, unprepared individual who complicates his ignorance with obstinacy. Of course, this can be carried only so far. The more informed party may simply call off the negotiation, if his bargaining position permits, or refuse to continue the negotiations until a more informed opponent is provided.

A summary is a brief and comprehensive presentation of the facts, statements or agreements reached at the negotiation. The majority of negotiations cover many points and last for a considerable period of time. The summations are the devices by which the negotiation is "packaged."

In lengthy negotiations covering many issues, summaries and conclusions may be required at transitional points throughout the negotiation. The number of transitional or intermediate summaries required in the negotiation depends chiefly on the length and complexity of the items discussed. It may also depend upon the experience and abilities of the negotiators on each side.

Intermediate summaries should definitely be used in two cases. When you have reached a conclusion and resolved a major point of issue during the negotiation, take the time to summarize the agreement and, if necessary, to put it in writing. You should also make a summary when a major issue has been analyzed exhaustively but cannot be resolved, so is being left until later in the same negotiation period or perhaps deferred for consideration at a later date. To avoid going over the same ground in the future, make a summary of the discussion, the points that have been agreed to, the points upon which no agreement has been reached, and the method by which both sides will review the issue. When negotiations last over several days, a summary should be developed at the end of each day's session, to outline the accomplishments of the day. A summary becomes even more important if the negotiation is recessed for a period of time. Negotiators for both the buyer and the seller may change, or individual team members may change. Therefore, it is important that the agreements reached be summarized and that the areas of disagreement be clearly defined so that it will not be necessary to repeat any work when the negotiation commences.

Summaries may be used to gloss over or to omit any undesirable points raised by the other side. If the other side agrees with the summary, it makes a concession by default. Summaries may also emphasize desirable points raised by the other side. However, the biggest value of summaries is that they insure understanding between the two parties about the status of negotiations and about any interim agreements.

In this summaries technique, which can be used by both buyer and seller, one member of a negotiation team takes an extreme position while another assumes the actual position on which the team hopes to reach agreement. By contrast, the actual position appears far more moderate than the extreme position, and its advocate, more conciliatory than his colleague. The conciliatory team member is able to win his opponent's confidence, and as his position seems comparatively reasonable, his chances of securing agreement from the other party are materially increased.

A tactic primarily used by government negotiators, with varying degrees of success, involves an appeal to the seller's emotions by references to his patriotism, the national importance of the procurement, and the seller's human desire to be liked. When the buyer tries this, the seller should remind him of Samuel Johnson's statement, "Patriotism is the last refuge of a scoundrel." Johnson meant that a person who attempts to use patriotism for his own selfish purposes is behaving unpatriotically. If the appeal is couched in terms of "Don't you want the agency to like you?" the contractor's response should be, "For how much?"

A common technique used by both buyer and seller is to raise straw issues and then concede them after lengthy discussion. Some sellers may deliberately inflate their quotation with semivisible soft spots that they expect the buyer to discover and remove for example, excessive overhead rates, exorbitant profit factors, duplicate charges for scrap and salvage, inconsistent accounting practices, and so forth. After removing the soft spots, the buyer may be satisfied that he has accomplished something and so may be less disposed to demand further concessions from the seller. He also has something tangible to show to his superiors. For his part, the seller appears reasonable and conciliatory when he agrees to negotiate the inflated areas out of his quotation.

As a slight variation on this tactic, during negotiations a seller may make a great to-do about an issue that is, in fact, relatively unimportant to him. He will argue at length, bring in experts to support his position, recess several times to reconsider, and then finally concede on a point that he intended to concede all along. This approach not only builds up the seller's claim that he has compromised in an effort to seek negotiation agreement but, more important, it wastes time and may weaken the buyer's bargaining position.

The buyer can counter the contractor's use of the straw issue technique by:

1. Making adequate prenegotiation preparations that effectively analyze the seller's quotation and reveal his true negotiation objectives
2. Maintaining effective communications control and adhering to a predetermined agenda during the conduct of actual negotiations.

The buyer can use the same tactics in reverse, by:

1. Making an extremely low offer on individual issues
2. Raising a large number of questions in his fact finding that he does not intend to press during the negotiation
3. Taking strong stands on issues that he fully intends to concede, or taking strong positions where the contractor least expects them.

Ultimate use of the straw issue technique occurs when one party is able to trade its concessions on a straw issue for the other party's compromise on a real one.

Tactical use of recesses may often prove advantageous during negotiations. A recess may restore communications control when a team member gets out of line. It may help to re-create a cordial, unemotional bargaining atmosphere if tempers flare. A recess may be beneficial in dealing with people who become increasingly intractable with fatigue. Recesses may be used by both sides to divert the discussion from areas in which they are weak or to get off the defensive. Experience has proven that after a recess, discussions very rarely start up precisely where they left off, so that by diligent post-break summaries of the discussions to date, the negotiator can often steer around sensitive areas or issues.

The opposite technique is to keep the negotiation going through the night. This technique is often used by sellers, especially those who are negotiating at the buyer's office. They have nothing to do but sit around a motel at night, so they want to spend as much time as possible in settling the issue. In other cases, sellers use the technique in the hope that fatigue or anxiety to close out the negotiation will cause the buyer to concede points that he may otherwise not concede. This is a bad tactic. First, negotiation requires preparation. It should be conducted during normal business hours; this allows time at the beginning and end of the day for recapitulation and planning. Further, when both sides grow tired, they are bound to say things and to take positions that they would not do if their faculties were operating at full power.

Under certain circumstances, it may be advisable for either or both sides to consider changing the individual team members, or even the principal negotiators. This may be advisable, for example, if one side decides that the other side's representatives are so superior in knowledge of the particular topic or in negotiation ability that substitution of a more qualified negotiator is necessary. It may also become necessary to change team members when a personality clash develops, making it extremely difficult, if not impossible, for the negotiation to continue in a proper frame of reference. This is not done so often as it should be, for each side blames the other for the bad relations and hesitates to make changes for fear of showing weakness.

In some cases, members of the negotiation team are changed in order to wear down the other side. This is a particularly effective technique for the buyer when the seller is adamant and refuses to compromise. Forcing him to restate his position a number of times in succession may weaken the seller's position and place him on the defensive. Further, as the seller repeats his position, discrepancies may develop that can be taken up and used to advantage in negotiation.

In some negotiations, threats are made by one of the parties. The seller can threaten to walk out and refuse to do business with the buyer. The buyer can threaten to close off the negotiation if the seller does not concede some point at issue. Normally, both sides stand to gain something by the negotiation or they would not be conducting it; therefore, it may be assumed that any threat contains elements harmful to both sides. Neither side has an incentive to behave in a way that will result in mutual harm, so logically, the person making the threat has no real incentive to carry it out. On the other hand, either side may have an incentive to make a threat on the basis that the threat itself may be successful if the other side has a strong stake in the negotiation and thinks that the threat may be carried out. Under those circumstances, the threat itself and not its fulfillment wins the goal. However, where each party's stake in the outcome of a negotiation is approximately equal, a threat may lack credibility from the beginning and rebound to the detriment of the person making it. The effectiveness of any threat is directly related to the strength of the belief of the other party that it will be carried out. The feelings of each side concerning the logic and rationality of the other will have a strong effect on whether or not a threat succeeds.

In some circumstances, the buyer can threaten to go to another source. If the seller knows from his own experience in making the item that this is impossible because of time limits, proprietary data, or if he knows as a result of the information he secured in the negotiation that he is the lowest cost producer, he will discount the threat on the grounds that it would do more harm to the buyer than to him. However, if such a threat is made by the buyer during the initial stages of the negotiation, while the seller knows that he is competing against a number of acceptable suppliers, the buyer's threat will probably be accepted at its face value.

Conversely, a threat by the seller to call off negotiations will lack credibility if the buyer knows that the seller desperately needs the business. But if the buyer knows that the seller's business is booming and his facility is operating at a high level of utilization, he will be more apt to accept the seller's threat at its face value.

Ordinarily, threats should not be used in a negotiation except in an attempt to reach a final resolution of all issues. By this time, however, both sides may be so committed that threats lack credibility. Further, if one side is represented by a stupid, obstinate person, the other side may feel that it is too risky to make threats since the uninformed party either may not recognize the seriousness of the threat or may not care.

Any threat made in negotiation must be realistic or it will reflect on the common sense of the person making it. Further, a threat should not be made unless the party making it has studied its possible effects on both parties.

All negotiations have some element of bluffing. Each side has a minimum position and a maximum position. Each will try to secure the maximum, but will accept the minimum if it becomes necessary. The minimum figure of the seller or the maximum figure of the buyer will be adjusted downward or upward based on the information secured in the negotiation. Under these circumstances, how does one party convince the other of its position? For example, suppose that a seller submits a proposal to do a job for $100,000. The buyer feels firmly that he should not pay more than $85,000.

How does the seller convince the buyer that he will not sell for less than $100,000? How does the buyer convince the seller that he will not pay more than $85,000?

All threats are bluffs unless the person doing the threatening is absolutely sure that he is going to carry out his threat. For example, suppose one party refuses to negotiate and adopts a take-it-or-leave-it attitude. The other side must consider whether he is bluffing or really means it. The situation is like two trucks loaded with dynamite that meet in the middle of a one-lane bridge. One of them has to back up. The question is which one. Ordinarily the party to back up has the most to lose or cares the least about the issue involved. Determining which party fits the description, is one of the major elements in any negotiation. A logical person will evaluate the odds and make a decision accordingly. To bluff requires both a streak of irrationality and the ability to analyze your opponent's reaction to a bluff. In the example of the dynamite trucks, for example, if both drivers are logical, they will discuss factors such as which can back up more easily. But assume that when the two men meet in the center of the bridge, one discovers that the other is a raving maniac. Then there is no question as to who will back up. If both are insane, the bridge is due for replacement. As with other types of threat, the effectiveness of any bluff is directly related to the strength of the belief of the other party that it will be carried out.

The buyer can try to give the seller the impression that a sole-source procurement situation is really a competitive one. If the seller has analyzed his bargaining position properly, he should be able to evaluate this accurately.

During negotiations, sellers often try to appear casual about their need or desire for a proposed contract. Most of the time, this is a negotiation technique aimed at improving a bargaining position. The buyer should always adopt the attitude that the presence of the seller at the negotiation table is positive evidence of his interest in and desire for the contract.

Another technique is to make negotiation difficult, perhaps by conducting negotiation by letter, or by sending a seller an offer that he may accept or reject. This puts tremendous pressure on the seller to accept rather than risk the loss of the order or to spend the time and associated costs in attempting to negotiate a better deal. One method of increasing the effectiveness of this technique is for the buyer to send the seller a letter making an offer effective only through a certain date and then to make himself unavailable for negotiation by going on vacation.

There are many types of bluffs in use. Either one or both parties can threaten to call off the negotiation. The buyer can threaten to go to another source or to issue only a small initial order to cover his immediate requirements pending the development of a second source. In addition, all of the following techniques that involve threats may be considered bluffs unless the threat will positively be carried out, if necessary.

Outright lies are used more often in negotiation than the average negotiator cares to admit. Obviously, neither side expects the other to tell the whole truth. If this were not so, then each would be expected to make known to the other all the information at its disposal, including its minimum and maximum positions. Such a procedure would make negotiation impossible. Distinguishing between proper negotiation "puffing" and outright lies is very difficult, if not impossible, because any such determination would undoubtedly reflect the sense of ethics of the person making it. Even highly ethical people may distinguish between a lie and a permissible negotiation technique based on whether they tell it or their opponent does. It is sad but true that often "Whose ox is getting gored" determines the rightness or wrongness of an action, rather than any fundamental criteria.

When the seller is adamant about compromising to a reasonable position, the buyer may threaten to keep other work from him. Normally, the seller is anxious for more work. He is usually more dependent on the buyer than the buyer is on him. Even if he is a sole source, the seller must consider future work not only for the facility involved but also for other divisions. He will rarely take a position on a single issue, even a large one, that may jeopardize his chances of getting other work.

Nonetheless, the seller should not take too seriously a threat by the buyer to withhold other work. Normally, the buyer's function is to negotiate the contract. This is particularly true in government. Source selection, not only for the contract under consideration but also for other work, is a function of a process involving a great many people within the technical and administrative areas of the buyer's operation. The buyer rarely has the ultimate authority to make decisions in this process. Even if he has, he probably would not exercise it because of a single negotiation disagreement, for he realizes that this is part of the game. This does not mean that contractors who refuse to negotiate or to compromise or who use a sole-source position to secure unreasonable objectives will not suffer the consequences. Eventually, such a seller's reputation will spread throughout the buyer's organization, making a definite impression on future source selection activities.

Buyers have a number of systems to evaluate a contractor's

performance during and after the completion of contract performance. These evaluations are used in future source selections and profit and fee determinations; they are made available to a renegotiation board. In the negotiation of various issues within the period of contract performance changes, extra work, terminations, and so on, a contractor may refuse to compromise, hoping he will wear the buyer down sufficiently to get his way. A threat to document the seller's obstinacy in a written evaluation generally puts him in a more reasonable frame of mind: a bad evaluation may cost him substantial contracts in the future.

Government agencies cannot blacklist a contractor except by means of the "Debarred and Ineligible Bidders List," use of which is carefully defined in the Armed Services Procurement Regulations. Private companies, however, can and do use a blacklist, although they will deny vehemently that they do.

The "Buyer's Guide" of many firms includes a list of firms with which the company has had difficulties in the past. The buyer may not buy from any of these firms without the express permission of senior purchasing management. Needless to say, buyers will usually go to great lengths to avoid buying from the listed companies. A veiled threat by a commercial buyer to put a firm on his list is always a serious matter, since often the firm will remain on the list for many years after the reason for the listing has been forgotten.

When he has the authority to do so, the buyer may threaten to issue a unilateral decision. This technique is possible in the negotiation of equitable adjustments for changes, termination claims, incentive contracts, and so on. In procurement, the buyer is entitled to do this under standard dispute clauses stating that any dispute concerning a question of fact arising under the contract that is not disposed of by agreement will be decided by the contracting officer, who will put his decision in writing and mail or otherwise furnish a copy to the contractor.

The decision of the buyer is final unless the seller appeals it within thirty days of its receipt. If the seller appeals the decision, he then receives a hearing. So, the obvious way for the seller to counter this threat by the buyer is to threaten to appeal. Buyer agencies do not like appeals. They represent a breakdown of the negotiation process and present the buyer's negotiator and the entire agency with a major administrative problem in preparing their case.

A buyer's negotiator can rarely issue such a decision on his own authority. Even if he is the buyer, he has to discuss the decision with his management, who are usually even more allergic to appeals than the buyer. Commercial firms are even more reluctant to engage in protracted law suits unless the issue is a major one.

If both sides recognize that negotiation is essentially compromise, there should be no necessity for the buyer to use such a technique. However, when the issue is important and compromise is impossible, it may be the only solution.

Under certain circumstances, it may be to the seller's advantage to request a formal decision and findings from the buyer from which to take an appeal. This may be necessary if the buyer delays negotiation or takes an adamant position on a major issue that may have serious effects on the seller, such as delaying payments for changes, extra work, or termination claims. To bring this issue to a head, the seller should request a decision and findings under a dispute clause upon which to make a formal appeal. If the buyer will not give him one, the seller can file a formal appeal addressed to management and forward it through the buyer. When this happens, the buyer will probably take the position that the seller had no right to appeal because no decision had been rendered by the buyer officer under the disputes clause of the contract. The seller can then take a position that the buyer's failure to act is, in the circumstances, a decision.

Under the guidelines, the buyer must forward all appeals to the management within ten days, whether or not he considers them justified. The net result of this approach would probably be the buyer's issuing a formal decision and findings in return for the seller's withdrawing his appeal, pending a proper appeal based on the buyer's decision. It is not a recommended technique: this type of pressure negotiation leads to acrimonious debates and hard feelings that may seriously affect the seller's present and future relations with the agency involved.

Under certain conditions, such as in negotiations to complete letter contracts and change orders, the seller or the buyer can allow the issue to drag out. If, as a result of a delay by the seller, the work is already performed, work will be priced on an after-the-fact basis and it should be priced at minimal-profit or fee rates. When the buyer uses a deliberate delaying tactic, a contractor can pursue the countertechnique, discussed above, of issuing a formal notice of appeal, even though he does not have a formal decision and findings upon which to base the appeal.

One method of putting pressure on a buyer is to threaten to notify a renegotiation board. This is not too effective a threat, because the contracting officer is required by policy to file renegotiation performance records that include information concerning the reasonableness of cost and profits earned by the seller. However, the threat may prove effective if the board has recovered funds from the seller in past years. However, the board is concerned only with profits on government business, and then on an across-the-board basis rather than a contract-by-contract basis.

This technique is rarely used by buyers: the possibility of its backfiring is too great. The major purpose of audits is to survey the overall efficiency of procurement operations, so that calling in the auditor may result in a derogatory report concerning the efficiency of not only the individual contracting officer but also his entire agency. Rarely will this threat be followed up by action.

Another pressure tactic available to the buyer is to threaten to audit the company heavily during performance of the contract work. The buyer has the right to audit, on an after-the-fact basis, fixed-price redeterminable and incentive contracts and all cost-type contracts. For firm fixed-price contracts, the audit and records clause gives the buyer the right to examine the books, records, documents, papers, and other supporting data involving transactions related to the contract sufficient to permit adequate evaluation of the cost or pricing data submitted. This right to audit applies only to those contracts on which certified cost and pricing data were submitted. The same cost and pricing data requirements provide that the buyer is entitled to an adjustment of a negotiated price including profit or fee to exclude any significant sum by which the price was increased because of the submission of defective data. Therefore, the threat to audit is a serious one, since rarely, if ever, can the contractor be sure that an audit would not develop discrepancies in his estimate that could be the basis of a future price reduction.

When an impasse is reached, the issue can be sent upstairs to the top management of the buyer and the seller. This may end in a conference in which the blind lead the blind, so it is a dangerous tactic for both sides. It is also an admission by one or both negotiators that he cannot perform his job without the assistance of top management. More dangerously, top management may end up by making unwarranted concessions harmful to their own positions, as they rarely understand either specific details or the nuances of the negotiation sufficiently to make an effective decision.

There are two methods of negotiation, sequential and overall. In sequential negotiation, both parties reach firm agreement on each issue before moving to another. In overall negotiation, the parties discuss each issue but reach no final conclusion on any one except as part of a final package. Obviously, the latter method is better: it prevents the negotiation from stalemating on individual issues that probably can be resolved or compromised when the objectives of both sides are fully identified. It is difficult, therefore, to see what reason either the buyer or the seller has to walk out of a negotiation until the objectives of both sides have been completely developed and the issues clearly identified—unless, of course, one side displays a completely adamant attitude and refuses to negotiate at all. Under those circumstances, it may be necessary for either the seller's or the buyer's team to walk out. However, this is very difficult to do effectively, so this technique should be used only when it can be backed up or when the negotiator is skillful enough to change his mind gracefully.

In the final stages of the negotiation, a walkout by the buyer's team may lead the seller to believe that his latest offer will not be accepted, that he is not a sole source for the procurement, or that the buyer will cancel or change the requirement unless he is willling to compromise. If it does this, it is a successful technique. But if the seller correctly evaluates his bargaining position and determines that the buyer must deal with him, the walkout will fail, wasting valuable contracting lead time, making a reconciliation between the parties difficult, and otherwise weakening the buyer's position because an extreme negotiation tactic has failed.

The same conditions apply even more emphatically to a walkout by the seller. Again, this should be carried out only at the very last stages in the negotiation, when both sides have clearly stated their objectives and have been able to analyze within reasonable ranges the targets that each is after. In some cases, inexperienced sellers, particularly senior managers unfamiliar with the concept and techniques of negotiation, may lose their tempers and walk out of a negotiation. When the buyer feels that a walkout by the seller is imminent, it may be advisable for him to try to forestall it. He can do this by suggesting a recess until lunch or for the balance of the day. If the issue is a major one, he can suggest a longer break while the parties go back to think things over and review their positions.

Before walking out of a negotiation, each side should consider its position very carefully. If the negotiations have progressed to any degree at all, the buyer and the seller know that they must deal with each other: the buyer, because the seller is in a sole source position or has been selected on the basis of overall analysis to receive the contract; and the seller, because ordinarily he wants the contract, and a single issue is rarely important enough to justify the loss of the contract. Under the circumstances, both sides should consider their positions very carefully before taking such an extreme step.

A walkout should never be staged as part of a temper tantrum. This ploy is for children, not for adults. If a walkout is considered necessary by either side, a short recess should be called, and when the negotiation reconvenes, the side that intends to call off the negotiation should clearly and carefully explain the basis for its action. Both negotiators should remain friendly and express willingness to reopen negotiations and to reconsider their overall positions before reopening negotiations at a specified date in the future. The threat of a walkout is an extreme tactic that more often than not boomerangs. When a walkout is threatened, neither side should panic, become angry, or, even worse, show weakness by making unwarranted compromises. Making concessions is an orderly process based on reason and persuasion; never make concessions under duress.

13 Propositions

This chapter consists of a series of propositions about negotiation. This series makes a systematic presentation in an explicit manner of a large number of ideas. Many propositions and observations may seem self-evident to the reader. This is intentional. Stating the self-evident in a clear, concise, and unambiguous way allows the reader to evaluate whether the obvious is necessarily correct. Further, what is obvious to one reader is not necessarily obvious to another. Last, a systematic structure of ideas must include the obvious, or the structure will have important gaps.

Some readers may have difficulty with this approach, wishing that the general statements were clarified with specific examples. This lack is also deliberate. It is designed to force the reader to analyze the validity of the propositions in relation to his own experience.

1. The term "negotiation or bargaining" may be used to refer to negotiation among buyers and sellers concerning the relative distribution of gains, burdens, and risks among themselves.

2. Negotiation is the use of debate and persuasion not to win an argument but to resolve issues—not individual issues, but the whole problem.

3. Negotiation is not a process of giving in or mutual sacrifice in order to secure agreement. It is an attempt to find a formula that will maximize the interests of both parties.

4. A negotiator must always remember that he is attempting to win his points, but not necessarily to cause his opponent to lose his.

5. When the interests of both parties are wholly in conflict, or are completely overlapping, there is no room for negotiation. In the first situation, the parties are concerned exclusively with reaching agreement and coordination.

6. The distinction between a conflict situation and a cooperative one is indicated by a greater willingness of the two parties to be flexible in their approach to the problem, or even to make generous concessions in the areas in which they have common interests.

7. When the negotiators foresee only divergence of interests or conflict of interests in the negotiation, and make no attempt to develop and to understand elements of common interest to both sides, either one or both may be unwilling or unable to negotiate properly and will fail to do justice to the full range of his interest.

123

8. The essence of successful negotiation is to convince the other side that it can gain more by accepting a compromise than by having a test of strength, for victory is more often won in the mind of a competitor than in the economic arena. The personal element is crucial in negotiation, which is rarely a straightforward analytical process. It starts as a mutually advantageous exchange of values. When a really attractive deal is formulated, both parties stand to gain if they agree to it, while both stand to lose if they do not. The real object of the negotiation is to decide who will benefit more.

9. If the relative bargaining strength of one party is overwhelming, negotiations may not take place, even though the session is formally classified as a negotiation session. Under the circumstances, the stronger party may feel that it can dictate the terms and, therefore, that it does not need to negotiate. Likewise, the weaker party may recognize its inferior position and concede to the stronger. When the negotiation strength of two parties is relatively equal, there may be a delay in the negotiation while each party attempts to improve its bargaining position.

10. A negotiation may be a single completely integrated combination of tactics and procedures. Often, however, a negotiation is only one element in an entire relationship between the buyer and the seller. Each party is aware that there have been negotiations in the past and that there will be other relationships in the future. The effect of a specific action on future relations may limit either side's use of a strong bargaining position in a specific procurement action. The desire by both parties to protect a long-term relationship has a significant impact upon any negotiation. If both parties view a specific negotiation not in its individual context but as a single exercise in the overall framework of a continuing relationship, their approach to the negotiation will be significantly similar. Both sides will be less inclined to seek a total victory over their opponent if they realize that there will be other negotiations and other chances. For example, in the initial negotiation of a contract, the seller may make concessions in the hopes that the buyer may make future concessions with references to specification changes, delivery schedules, equitable adjustments for changes, and so on. The buyer may make concessions to maintain good relations with an efficient supplier.

11. When there is continuous negotiation between two parties, learning and adaptation takes place. Each party becomes familiar with the strategy and the tactics of the other. Parties that start out either friendly or antagonistic toward each other may find the situation reversed as learning and adaptation take place. One party may become familiar with the strategy and tactics of the other, or

may recognize the problems and specific areas of concern of the other; therefore, reaching a settlement may be eased.

12. In negotiation, the strongest party does not always win, and the outcome does not always reflect the relative bargaining position of each side. Many factors effect the outcome of a negotiation, and a settlement is reached only when a number of factors equaling the minimum positions of both sides are agreed to. It is assumed in negotiation that each side is seeking to reach an agreement; however, the minimum terms acceptable to each side may prevent an agreement, regardless of how interested both parties are in reaching that agreement.

13. Power is not necessarily strength in negotiation. The terms "bargaining power," "bargaining strength," and "negotiation skill" may suggest that the advantage in negotiation goes to the powerful, the strong, or the skillful. These terms imply that it is advantageous to be intelligent, more logical, better informed, or better off financially. This is not necessarily true in negotiation. A truly sophisticated negotiator may find it extremely difficult to take an illogical position (which he cannot support) in a negotiation; but a stupid, uninformed, obstinate negotiator may take and stand firmly on erroneous positions because he knows no better.

14. Though both parties to a negotiation usually claim that they want to reach agreement, this is not necessarily always the case. Negotiations may be initiated for a variety of other purposes, including delay, deception, diversion, or exploration. This is particularly true in negotiations leading to the settlement of letter contracts, changes, or termination claims. In these cases, the buyer, though seemingly seeking an agreement, may be interested in delaying negotiations until more cost data is available. The seller, however, may also be interested in delaying negotiations, because he is operating in a cost-plus environment and does not want to reach agreement. In other cases, either the buyer or the seller or both may delay the negotiation, hoping that the other party will become impatient to reach a settlement and increase its offer. Negotiations entered into for such secondary purposes may serve the purpose of one or both of the parties but very seldom produce a settlement of the points at issue. Negotiations of this type are more accurately classified as fact-finding sessions; however, it may be to the interests of both parties to classify them as negotiation sessions.

15. Fact finding is useful for exploratory purposes. It is used to establish whether the parties are ready for serious bargaining, and it may also play a role in determining the limits within which explicit bargaining may usefully proceed.

16. In planning for negotiation, both sides should decide not only the strategy, tactics, and techniques they will use but also any maneuvers that can be made outside of the negotiation itself to affect the outcome.

17. The extent of the considerations that may affect a negotiation indicate the wide range of strategy, tactics, and maneuvers open to each party in trying to influence the outcome of the negotiation.

18. Some bargaining techniques are more effective in a single negotiation between negotiators than they are if the negotiators have previous experience in dealing with each other. This is particularly true with techniques involving bluffing, which becomes less effective as it becomes more familiar. Each side will develop counters to the more familiar techniques used by the other side.

19. It is absolutely essential to know the character, attitudes, motives, and habitual behavior of a competitor if you wish to have a negotiating advantage.

20. Each party in a negotiation will normally try to secure the most favorable outcome for itself that it believes will be acceptable to the other party. However, while each party tries to gain at the expense of the other, it is assumed that each has an interest in trying to reach some agreement.

21. Negotiation normally consists of a mixture of common and conflicting interests. In order to negotiate at all, each party to the negotiation must feel that it has something to gain by negotiation and may have something to lose by failing to negotiate. In this type of situation, the total gain or total loss depends upon the actions of both the parties.

22. One of the major purposes of negotiation is to convince the other side that either his short- or long-range interest will benefit by accepting the first party's position, or that he has failed to evaluate properly all of the options and that the position presented by the first party is fairer and more equitable to both sides than the one he is presenting.

23. You must know as accurately as possible just what your competition has at stake in his contact with you. It is not what you gain or lose, but what he gains or loses that sets the limit on his ability to compromise with you.

24. The less the competition knows about your stakes, the less advantage he has. Without a reference point, he does not even know whether you are being unreasonable.

25. On one hand, the demands presented by both parties at the outset of a negotiation may represent the result desired by each party, but not necessarily the expected one. On the other hand, the

initial positions of both sides may represent nothing more than bargaining positions in which the seller sets his maximum position extremely high and the buyer sets his minimum offer very low, solely to allow themselves room to maneuver. The more precise the statement of work and the fewer contingencies inherent in the contract, the closer the initial positions of both parties should be.

26. Skill in negotiating consists of being as arbitrary as necessary to obtain the best of the deal without destroying the basis for cooperation. In bargaining, the negotiator should make sure that the other side fully understands what he has to win and to lose from the deal. He should not arouse emotional responses on the other side: it is necessary that he act in a logical, rational way. He must convince the opponent that he is emotionally dedicated to his position and is convinced that it is reasonable. Neither side to a negotiation should take completely arbitrary positions, for if they do, the negotiation will break down.

27. The more arbitrary your demands, the better your relative competitive position—provided that you do not arouse an emotional reaction.

28. The less arbitrary you can appear, the more arbitrarily you can act.

29. The less rational or less predictable the behavior of a competitor appears to be, the greater advantage he possesses in establishing a favorable competitive balance, provided that he avoids forcing competitors into an untenable position or creating an emotional response that will lead them to be more unreasonable and irrational than he.

30. Arbitrary positions that are mutually exclusive become an absolute obstacle unless compromised. If both parties are irrational, an agreement is impossible. However, if one party is really irrational and the other side realizes it but is not itself irrational, then the agreement will be reached on the irrational party's terms.

31. When the negotiation has reached a point where both sides have something to gain and something to lose if the negotiation falls through, the agreement reached will basically depend on three considerations: each side's willingness to accept the loss involved; each side's judgement as to the other side's willingness to accept the loss involved; and both sides' evaluation of the rationality of their opponent.

32. There are three rules of behavior. Be as cooperative as possible and minimize emotional responses and arbitrary behavior. Be stubborn in the attitudes you take. This will convince the other side that you are determined to have your way. Be as friendly and responsive as possible, and leave the possibility of compromise open if necessary.

33. In some cases, the ultimate solution may be obvious. In other cases, there may be a number of available solutions. In many cases there is no single obvious solution for either side but a number of solutions on a linear scale that may be acceptable to both sides.

34. The best or most logical solution may not be clear to both parties at the outset of a negotiation. However, it may become the only solution available as negotiation proceeds.

35. The logical solution to a specific negotiation may not necessarily be the best solution or the fairest. It is simply the solution that each party believes the other will agree to as the logical solution.

36. Normally, a negotiation proceeds by successive discussions of individual issues until at least one party feels that the gap has been closed sufficiently to enter into serious negotiations to reach a final agreement. The extent of the concessions made by each party during the negotiation are related to bargaining position. There are three bargaining positions in each negotiation: what the buyer thinks his bargaining position is in relationship to the seller; what the seller thinks his bargaining position is in relation to the buyer; and an objective evaluation of the bargaining position of both sides. One of the major objectives of negotiation is to determine the relative bargaining position of both sides. In this context, the term "bargaining position" refers not only to the actual bargaining position of both sides but also to what each thinks the other's bargaining position is.

37. As the negotiation continues, it is expected that one or both parties will change positions in order to secure agreement.

38. In some cases, a party to a negotiation will attempt to convince the other party that it cannot make a concession when, in fact, it can. Of course, this can be effective only when one negotiator is able to convince the other negotiator that he does not have the authority to make concessions. In some cases, this can be achieved only by management's actually placing constraints on the concessions that may be made, and in some manner demonstrating to the other party that the constraints are really there. This can be accomplished by restricting the negotiator's authority to negotiate certain issues beyond a minimum figure. This is rather drastic, because it is a take-it-or-leave-it position that, if not carried through, may destroy the negotiator's position on other issues. It leaves little room for retreat, so if the other side takes an adamant position, negotiations may break down.

39. One single issue is rarely important enough to justify the breakdown of a negotiation.

40. In protracted negotiations, both sides tend to attach progressively more importance to the positions they have taken, particularly the positions that are in major conflict with the other side.

Negotiators may even attempt to attribute ethical and moral justification to their positions. When this is not done as a deliberate tactic, it is a sign of immaturity and lack of emotional control. Such positions make agreement much more difficult to achieve. If, however, this is done intentionally to achieve an irrational or intransigent image in the mind of the other party, it may be a useful tactic.

41. A stalemate results when the parties commit themselves to incompatible objectives or when one party makes the mistake of committing itself to a position that the other side cannot or will not accept. Once a stalemate is reached, both parties have an interest in removing the obstacle. However, the interests of the two sides will differ as to the method of resolving the stalemate. One of the best methods, of course, is not to make unfortunate commitments in the first place. The second method applies to a stalemate on an individual issue. It is to recognize that agreement on individual issues is not necessary, as it may be possible to reach agreement in other areas of negotiation that will render the stalemated issue inconsequential.

42. In many cases, negotiators attempt to justify their demands on the basis of past precedents. This is particularly true in the areas of profit percentages, acceptance of bidding rates, average labor rates, past improvement curves, and so on. Normally, both sides attempt to justify their positions on past precedents, if they are available. However, each issue should be decided on its own merits.

43. Normally, concessions will be made first on those issues that have been deliberately inflated for the purpose of negotiation, or in those areas that are marginal to the party's interests.

44. When a point is reached in negotiation where it is necessary to make concessions, the person making the concession must recognize that it will have two effects. First, it will put him closer to his opponent's position; second, it will affect his opponent's estimate of his firmness. A concession may be considered a capitulation or it may make the opponent think that the original firm commitment to the issue was a fraud. It may also make the other negotiator question the firmness of commitment to the remaining issues between the parties and encourage him to increase his demands. Therefore, concessions should be rationalized as a reinterpretation or reanalysis of the original commitment that is persuasive to the other side.

45. In some cases, concessions by one party to the other may facilitate agreements; however, the effect of the concession is determined by the basis on which the concession was made and the interpretation the other side makes of the concession. If a concession is interpreted as a sign of weakness, it may cause the other party to strengthen its demands, thereby making an agreement more difficult or impossible to reach. Therefore, concessions should be

made in an orderly fashion and in a manner demonstrating that they are made to facilitate agreement and not from weakness. If a concession is not regarded by the other side as a sign of weakness, then the party making the concession normally expects a concession in return.

46. In negotiation, each party attempts to convince the other that the concessions it is making are far more important to the second party than they actually may be. In addition, of course, each side attempts to mislead the other as to the minimum terms that it will accept.

47. In some cases, it is necessary for one party to a negotiation to assist his opponent in retreating from an initial commitment, by demonstrating that he has not actually made a firm commitment, or that he has miscalculated the effect of the commitment on his opponent. When it is obvious that the other side would like to make a concession on a specific area, but is reluctant to do so because of the firmness of its initial commitment, or because of fear that it will affect the other side's belief in the firmness of its remaining commitments and issues, the negotiator for the other side may help by suggesting that a concession is not only consistent with his previous position, but may even be called for by that particular position, and therefore that a concession will not affect the initial principles upon which the commitment was made. It is easier for an opponent to make a concession if he is assured that the concession will not be considered a reflection on his original credibility, or on his credibility with respect to the firmness of his commitment to the remaining portion of his positions.

48. When an agreement is reached on an important issue on which the two parties have been in conflict, it is generally a sign that the party making the concession makes it rather than have the negotiations fail altogether.

49. In the final stages of negotiation, it is sometimes necessary to convince the other side that you have made all the concessions you intend to make and that the responsibility for closing the deal rests upon his making a decision. There is a doctrine in law of the "last clear chance"; it recognizes that when an accident occurs there is some point at which the accident becomes inevitable, as the result of prior actions, and that the abilities of the two parties to prevent the accident may not expire at the same time. In many negotiation cases, the range of negotiation authority of one party may expire before that of the other party. It may be an effective negotiation technique to point this fact out to the opposing party and to convince him that he has the "last clear chance" to save the negotiation.

50. Some basic rules of negotiation follow:

1. Negotiation is a physical act. Its direction is a mental process. The better your strategy, the easier it will be for you to gain your objective.

2. The tougher your methods, the more bitter you will make your opponent, with the natural result of hardening his resistance.
3. If you are not absolutely certain of your ground, too extreme an approach will make your opponent's superiors close ranks behind him.
4. The more you try to impose your own way entirely, the stiffer the obstacles you will raise in your path.
5. The more you ask, the more trouble you will have, and the more cause you will provide for changing the result or for the other party to take reprisals in the future.
6. You must keep a line of retreat open on any position you take.
7. It is necessary to provide your opponent with a line of retreat or with a ladder to get him off a limb if he finds himself out on one. You can do this with a well-calculated compromise that shows no sign of weakness on your part or by presenting an alternative objective.

51. A contract is a statement of the comparative bargaining positions of both sides on the date on which it is signed. No matter how carefully a contract is drafted, there is always a question of interpretation. One of the major post award administrative problems is determining the distinction between an administrative interpretation to which both sides agree and a change that entitles the contractor to an equitable adjustment. Because of the vagueness of the scope of work of many contracts, the only thing that really makes an agreement enforceable is the recognition that if both parties do not act in an equitable, trustworthy manner, opportunities for future agreement within the same contract and agreements on other contracts will be eliminated. Normally, each party to a negotiation must be convinced that its long-term relationship is more valuable to the other party than an opportunity to take advantage in an individual instance.

14 The Session

When the two teams get together for the actual negotiation, the first test of strength will probably be on the seating arrangements. Because the buyer is generally the host, he is responsible for the arrangements. Many concerns and government agencies have very poor facilities for their buyers. Frequently, buyers or negotiators are quartered in loft-like areas, and the negotiation takes place around the buyer's desk. Major negotiations, however, generally take place in conference rooms. Wherever possible, regardless of the size or nature of the negotiation, both sides should try to see that the rooms and the seating arrangements are conducive to effective negotiation.

In many cases, the buyer assumes the roll of leader of the negotiation. This is perfectly proper, so long as he does not attempt to fill the places of both judge and jury. The buyer may seat himself at the end of the table, placing his team members on one side and the seller's negotiators on the other. The seller should not tolerate this type of arrangement; the seller's principal negotiator should sit directly facing the buyer.

Occasionally, the buyer attempts to scatter his team members—price analysts, engineers, and legal personnel—on both sides of the table while he remains at the end. Under no circumstances should the seller agree to this seating arrangement. It is not unheard of for the buyer's representatives to attempt to read over the seller's team's shoulders to determine their position. Of course, this is a two-edged sword. Some negotiators have even developed the ability to read upside down.

Some unscrupulous negotiators may go even farther in attempting to gain an advantage. They try to make their opponents physically uncomfortable by providing uncomfortable chairs. They also make sure that the other representatives face the window so that the light dazzles them. At the same time, these negotiators sit with their backs to the light, which allows them to see the faces of their opponents while their own are in shadow. When attempts such as these are noticed, the party against whom they are used should protest immediately and refuse to negotiate further until the conditions causing them discomfort are changed.

The best seating arrangement is to have the teams face each other

133

down the sides of an oblong table; principle negotiators for each side face each other, flanked by their respective team members. The team members should be paired off on opposite sides of the table: price analyst with price analyst, legal counsel with legal counsel, engineer with engineer, and so on.

The actual negotiation between the two parties should be divided into two parts. The first is fact finding; the second is the negotiation itself. The fact-finding sessions may be conducted with all members of both teams present. In large negotiations, however, the fact finding may be conducted by separate committees, which discuss the various technical, cost, and legal issues assigned to them. Their findings are then referred to the principal negotiators for each side, who have the ultimate responsibility for reaching agreement.

During the buyer's preliminary planning for the negotiation session, he should use all the devices available to him to determine the reasonableness of the seller's proposal. From this analysis, he should develop tentative objectives and minimum and maximum positions on the issues that he thinks will arise in the negotiation. However, he should not begin the negotiation immediately, since he does not know if the assumptions on which he bases his objectives and the selections of his issues are realistic. First he must determine that his analysis of the seller's proposal is correct. If he does not check the realism of the issues and the negotiation objectives that he has selected, he may find later that he has misunderstood the seller's proposal or that he has been furnished incomplete or erroneous information by his assistants. He will be forced to withdraw or to change his position early in a negotiation, which will weaken his position during the rest of the negotiation.

The purpose of the fact-finding session, therefore, is to check inconsistencies between the buyer's and the seller's cost information and inconsistencies in or misunderstandings of the seller's proposal. The majority of the inconsistencies are based on the individual cost elements that make up the price or the cost estimate, such as the number of labor hours, the types of labor used, and the projection of labor and overhead rates. During this period, the buyer should be careful not to reveal to the seller his position on various issues. The areas in which the buyer finds problems are obvious to the seller, but the buyer's position is not. By keeping his objectives and his analysis of the proposal to himself at this point, the buyer protects himself. Later, if the facts developed in the fact-finding session cause him to change his position, he will be able to change without embarrassment.

During the fact-finding session, the buyer generally uses detailed questions to secure information on specific points in the seller's proposal. The buyer may also ask broad, general, or ambiguous questions in the hopes that he will bring out unsolicited information from the seller. The seller must keep in mind that at this stage of the game, he should be completely defensive. Many buyers simply ask the seller to justify each cost element in his proposal, hoping that they will be able to catch the seller in an inconsistency. If the buyer's questions develop vague or veiled answers, he may then probe deeper into the particular area by rephrasing the question, by using a different approach, or by postponing it and coming back to it later.

The buyer's strategy in the fact-finding session is one of a concealed offensive. He should keep his questions factual and ask them in a conversational tone; once he has asked a question, he should listen carefully and analyze the answer. During this period, however, the seller should answer only direct questions and confine his answers to the absolute minimum. During this stage, the redirected question becomes the seller's best defensive weapon. It is important to remember that the person who asks the questions has the initiative, and not simply the person who is talking.

Negotiation should not start until the issues to be negotiated have been thoroughly defined by both parties. Therefore, during the fact-finding part of the session, no counterarguments should be made by either side to points made by the other. This is extremely important because you are not yet negotiating, and you may find yourself revealing your position or wasting arguments at the beginning stages of negotiation that may be valuable to you later. If you advance your arguments too early, the opposition may turn them against you at a later and more important stage in the negotiation.

During this period, both parties should make an attempt to analyze the other party's point of view. The seller should attempt to determine from the questions asked by the buyer, and the buyer, from the answers and attitude of the seller, the importance the other side attaches to the issues involved. During this period, both sides engage in initial feeling-out processes to determine the attitudes and ability of the opposing team.

The buyer should continue his fact finding until he has a complete understanding of the seller's proposal, has established realistic issues, and has secured sufficient information to determine his position. If his fact finding has been conducted skillfully, he has also determined the basis of the seller's position and the strength of the seller's probable stands on particular issues. The seller should have a list of all the issues raised by the buyer; but, if the fact finding has been skillfully conducted, the seller does not know the relative importance that the buyer places on the individual issues.

At this point, a recess is in order. In a small procurement, the recess may be a short period of time for each team member to discuss the points developed in the fact-finding session with the other members of his team, to revise issues, positions, and to develop the strategy and tactics that will be used in the actual negotiation. In a major negotiation, this recess may last several weeks.

Both sides now have a fairly good idea of the important issues in the negotiation and the positions that each side will probably take. In addition, each should have a fair idea of the negotiating ability, the team integration, and the knowledge of the proposal evidenced by the other negotiating group. The seller should have some idea of the extent of the actual cost and price data available to the buyer.

Since a negotiation session is essentially a conference, it needs an agenda. The agenda is based on the issues that make up the subject of the negotiation, and should be established by mutual agreement. A major test of strength in the negotiation may arise at this point: that is, whether the issues will be negotiated separately, with a resolution reached prior to moving to the next issue; or whether all the issues will be established on the agenda and negotiated one at a time, but with no final resolution of any until a final resolution of the entire package.

Negotiating one issue at a time is best for the buyer, because it enables him to conceal his strategy and tactics. Therefore, the seller should insist that the buyer outline or list all of the issues in the negotiation. The justification for this, of course, is that the negotiation occurs not to resolve individual issues but to reach an overall resolution of the entire problem or the entire contract. Another advantage of listing the issues is that the list enables the seller to secure additional information where it is required. On the other hand, the buyer should try to secure agreement on each issue prior to moving to the others, because this prevents the seller from trading off one issue against another. Obviously, it is advantageous to the seller not to reach agreement on any specific issue until he has some idea of the total extent of the concessions the buyer will demand of him. If the buyer is adamant and refuses to outline all of the issues in the negotiation, the seller is still not defeated. He can simply discuss each issue as advanced by the buyer but refuse to come to a definite conclusion or to give a definite answer until all the issues have been placed on the table.

The seller must remember that the buyer has prepared a list of the issues that he feels will be present in the negotiation, and has established his tactics with regard to how these issues will be presented. His strategy, of course, is an offensive one. The buyer has the following tactical alternatives: to approach the issues in order of importance; to put the least important ones first; to put the most difficult ones first; to put the easiest ones first; or to arrange and to present his issues so that when the seller makes a concession on one, he will have to make a concession on others to be consistent. If an agenda is established at the start of the negotiation, the seller will be in a better position to determine just which tactic the buyer is using.

Once the negotiation starts, the seller assumes his defensive-offensive strategy. The buyer takes the offensive by outlining his position on the various issues. He presents supporting points, logic, appeals to reason, and even, in the case of government buyers, appeals to patriotism, to encourage the seller to change his point of view. As each issue is presented, the buyer attempts to convince the seller that the buyer's position is sound and that the seller's interests will be protected, if not maximized, by agreeing with the buyer. On the other hand, the seller should attempt to convince the buyer of the validity of his position and the risks that he is taking at the price quoted for the procurement.

It is important not to belabor a point. Each side should explore alternative solutions. Each side should state its position in broad terms rather than specific ones. If the other side objects to a proposed approach, you can counter effectively by stating your objective, justifying its reasonableness, and asking your opponent how *he* would achieve your objective, or how your objective can be achieved without lessening his position. This is particularly important for the seller, because the buyer may be objecting only to the method, not to the end result. For example, negotiations often bog down on discussions of profit or fee. Many buyers have strong prejudices in favor of particular percentages of fee or against paying more than a specific percentage. The same buyers may be willing to negotiate contingency factors into various other cost elements, so long as the percentage of profit or fee on the estimate meets his criteria.

In rebutting a pricing position taken by the seller, it is generally better for the buyer to indicate to the seller that he can justify a certain percentage of his proposal. The buyer should not set an arbitrary figure or state that he is going to knock the figure down by a given percentage.

In pure bargaining, each party should follow mainly its expectations of what the other will accept. Since each side normally bases its position on its expectations of what the other side will do, this compounds the negotiation. For example, how is a final agreement reached? One side may finally have to make a concession because the other side will not. But on the other hand, the other side will not because it expects that the first side will, in fact, make a concession. So in some cases in negotiation, the ideas of both sides about the position of the other are self-justifying.

If an agreement on a particular issue cannot be reached, then it is important that neither negotiator beat his head against the wall. If all the issues have not been covered, then the points of difference should be summarized and the sides should agree to move to another issue. Each side should continually keep in mind that negotiation is a discussion of all issues in order to arrive at an evaluation of the extent of the total difference between the two parties. The actual negotiation does not start until both sides know the extent of the concessions that will be asked. When a particular issue cannot be resolved, the negotiation should move to another issue. Settlement of a subsequent issue may automatically settle the one upon which agreement could not be reached. It is important to keep moving.

Depending upon the order in which the issues are placed on the negotiation table, it may be necessary to switch tactics completely. For instance, if the issues are being considered in their order of importance, and if no agreement can be reached on major issues, it may be necessary to switch to lesser issues in order to develop a pattern of agreement. It is necessary that all aspects of each issue be negotiated. If this is not done, unresolved problems or remaining fringe areas may come to a head at later stages in the negotiation, when they may be more troublesome or require a renegotiation of the entire issue.

Neither side should finally agree to any one issue; it should agree only to a complete package. Tentative agreements may be made about how each issue will be resolved, but these should always include a provision that the agreements depend upon reaching reasonable agreements on later issues.

Normally at some stage in the negotiation, both sides realize that they will make a deal. Once this conclusion is reached, neither side has any real incentive to make further concessions. At this point, the negotiation becomes more difficult; and at this point, items other than price, such as future relations between the parties or delivery schedules, may prove the deciding factor as to who makes the concessions leading to an ultimate agreement. Under the circumstances, the agreement ultimately reached is necessarily a compromise of both positions. Each party may recognize that the other party would have made more concessions, if necessary, to reach agreement.

Neither side should compromise simply to shorten the negotiation. The purpose of negotiation is not to reach an agreement for agreement's sake, but to seek maximization of benefits to both parties. Each issue should be negotiated completely and thoroughly. Negotiators for both sides should take pride in their ability to develop logical, persuasive reasons for why the other side should agree with their positions. Making concessions is an orderly process based on reason and persuasion.

In the majority of cases, it soon becomes obvious as to which side has the strongest or most logical reasoning to support its position. If the fundamental basis of the negotiation is to arrive at a reasonable settlement fair to both parties, then at this point, the other side could be expected reasonably to change its position and to agree either wholly or partly with the other. If, however, bargaining strength is the major factor in the negotiation, then a negotiator may have to continue refusing to recognize the logic of the other person's position, even when it is completely apparent.

Negotiations vary depending upon the skill, attitude, and particular strategy and tactics used by both sides. Some negotiators use persuasion and logic. Others use a combination of methods, depending upon the importance of the issue under consideration. Negotiations have been likened to a card game or to a game of chess. Other comparisons stressing the differences between the two parties consider negotiation tactics in the form of battle terminology.

1. Direct an overwhelming assault from a strong position to put the adversary on the defensive. Make sure that you have calculated the odds correctly.
2. Take over the opponent's position. Anticipate his arguments and use them to support your own.
3. Scatter the forces of the opponent. Lay out as many points as possible and ask for proof. Keep up a continual attack on weak points and omissions.
4. Retreat. Back away from your own weak points. Concentrate on your strong points.
5. Skirmish. Bring up trivial crises in order to divert attention from your own weak points.
6. Draw the opposition's fire from your strong positions, or else some arguments may overwhelm you.
7. Bottle up your opponent by a series of questions and create dilemmas if possible. Force him into a situation where it is obvious he does not have the authority to make a decision, and must ask his superiors for advice. This weakens his status in the negotiation.
8. Evade traps. Ignore them, or, if the opposition is insistent, reverse the trap question and relay it, substitute another, pretend misunderstanding, or misinterpret the meaning of the question.
9. Conceal your true objective. Do not disclose your real objective or the total concessions that you want until you are ready.

10. Withhold reserves. Present your weakest point first, and when you have exposed the opponent's flank, move in with your strong points.

No one approach should be used in a negotiation. Whether to use a strong or a weak approach, whether to take the offense or the defense, depends on the particular environment of the negotiation and the particular issue under discussion. It is important, however, that the negotiator have the skill and objectivity necessary to enable him to modify his strategy, tactics, attitude, and approach to meet the particular needs of the procurement and to counter the particular strategy, tactics, and approach used by the other side.

The following is a list of general factors that may affect the outcome of a particular negotiation:

1. The relative bargaining position of each party
2. The extent of the preparation and maneuvers made by the parties prior to, or during, the negotiation
3. The negotiation skills, attitudes, and characteristics of the negotiation parties
4. The past and present relationships between the two parties
5. The strategy and tactics used by both sides
6. The size of the stakes involved
7. The extent to which the interests of the parties are compatible or conflicting
8. The extent of information that both sides have of the importance that each side attaches to the various elements of the negotiation
9. The general background and situation serving as the framework for the negotiation
10. The level at which the negotiation is taking place
11. The format of the negotiation
12. The location of the negotiation
13. The extent of the confidence that each party has in the good faith of the other
14. The extent of the interest of one or both parties in achieving a settlement.

After each issue has been negotiated completely, a recess should be called. The buyer then analyzes each issue and develops a counter-offer. If a reasonable compromise is possible, it can be suggested, but only if the buyer intends to remain firm; otherwise, he has simply granted a concession. The total of counteroffers on each issue is the total offer. On complex issues and large contracts, the first counteroffer should be conservative.

If the buyer and the seller are close, the first counteroffer may be made in total dollars. A total dollar offer should not be made at this stage unless the buyer is reasonably certain that this will establish a reasonable minimum offer. The buyer should remember that once a counteroffer is made, it establishes his minimum position, which combines with the seller's offer to establish the range within which agreement will be reached. After a total dollar offer is made, the negotiation should be based on total dollars, and the individual issues should be disregarded.

If wide differences exist, the buyer should review the negotiation, select those issues in which he has the strongest position, revise his tactics and techniques, and negotiate each issue again in an attempt to narrow the differences. This process continues until total dollars can be used.

Some negotiators question whether the buyer should make a counteroffer or insist that the seller revise his proposal and submit a lower one. Normally, this is a matter of bargaining strength. The seller would be wise to insist that the buyer make a counteroffer, because this will define the buyer's minimum position. Until he secures some figure from the buyer, the seller has no benchmark from which to determine the negotiation range within which the buyer is operating.

As the negotiation proceeds, each issue is brought out on the negotiation table, thoroughly analyzed, and discussed. Eventually, as a result of the negotiation, the crux of the negotiation is reached when each side reaches its objective. Usually, the buyer's objective is lower than that of the seller; however, this is not always true.

The difference between the buyer's objective and the seller's objective represents the most difficult part of the negotiation. If this difference is relatively small, the obvious answer is to compromise the different points of view. In other cases, the bargaining strength of either party may be used to secure an agreement at, or close to, its particular objective. For example, if the agreement on the total cost estimate is within approximately five percent, both sides have a basis for a fixed-price contract, and at this point, either compromise or bargaining strength may be used legitimately to resolve the issue.

On the other hand, if the objectives of the buyer and the seller are a considerable distance apart after negotiation of all issues involved, there may be no basis for a reasonable compromise. At this point, the sides must consider other alternatives. For example, if in the final stages of negotiation, the buyer and the seller are twenty percent apart in their evaluation of the reasonable cost for the procurement, the buyer may consider changing the type of contract to either a redetermination or an incentive contract and making a new offer based on the new type of contract. If a different type of contract is proposed and the seller suspects or knows that the buyer's estimate of the actual cost of performance is more reasonable than his own, the proposal may encourage him to change his position. A redetermination contract, downward only, allows the seller only the actual cost of his performance, and his dollar amount of profit is subject to negotiation at the conclusion of the contract. An incentive contract, though better for the seller than a redetermination contract, allows the seller to keep only a small portion of any savings that he may develop under the contract. Thus, the seller may find it more to his advantage to compromise to secure a firm fixed-price contract.

When it becomes obvious that the negotiation has reached its crux, the two sides should recess to prepare their final bargaining position. At this stage, the real "hard-nosed" bargaining begins: each side is fighting close to its own territory. Concessions usually are made only on a *quid pro quo* basis. The negotiation usually becomes quite heated as one side or the other presses for advantage. The buyer threatens to get another source. The seller insists that he will not sell at a loss. The principal negotiators threaten to go over each other's heads to the respective superiors. This type of discussion brings out the best or the worst in a negotiator. If he can become vehement without becoming obnoxious, if he can exhibit determination but not stubbornness, if he can apply his bargaining strength without leaving lasting wounds, and if he can gain a victory or take a defeat gracefully, he can consider himself a true negotiator.

Though negotiation is by definition a reasoning, logical process, it cannot be divorced from its economic aspects and from the bargaining strength of both sides. Ultimately, final resolution of the problem may rest on the bargaining strength of each party. This should be obvious to both sides, so there is no need to call attention to it at the bargaining table. In other words, the bargaining position of each side is the "ace in the hole"; the effective negotiator is one who gives the impression of negotiating logically and reasonably, even though the negotiation really will be settled by the bargaining strength that he has. This applies particularly to the seller, because this impression enables him to negotiate a settlement rather than to force one, thus preserving the good will of the buyer and maintaining a sound basis for future relationships.

Even if one side is sole source or sole buyer, economic conditions force the seller to take a contract at a less than favorable price, or a proprietary item or technical data in the possession of the seller forces the buyer to pay what he considers an unreasonable price, these positions should not be brought too openly into the negotiation. Too much pressure will have long-range effects on the relations of both parties that may offset immediate benefits.

In order to bring the negotiation to a final test, it may be necessary to find out if the other side has made its final concession. Here the technique of the "doorknob price" may prove useful. It can be used by either side, but assume that the seller elects to use it. He summarizes the negotiation to date with special emphasis on the concessions that he has already made, and states his "final" offer. If it is rejected, he then prepares to call off the negotiation. He may even get to the point of putting his hand on the doorknob, at which point he asks the buyer bluntly if he will accept this last offer. If the buyer is still adamant, the seller may actually leave. Or, if he believes that the buyer's offer is final, he may return to the table and accept it.

The doorknob technique is based on the theory that neither side knows whether or not the other has reached rock bottom until the other threatens to break off the negotiations and convinces the first that he means it. The technique requires skill in giving the proper impression, in evaluating bargaining position, and even more in retreating gracefully if the negotiator finds he had overestimated his own strength or underestimated either the bargaining position or the determination and courage of his opponent.

In some cases, the parties are either so stubborn or so evenly matched or think they are that no amount of logic, persuasion, or bargaining strength leads to agreement. It may be necessary to bring the negotiation to an ultimate test of bargaining strength and call it off. If the buyer is under pressure from his technical personnel to place the contract and to secure the item or services involved, or if there is a deadline on the delivery schedule beyond which other phases of a more important project may be sacrificed, the buyer may have to give in to the seller's demands. Likewise, if the buyer has alternative sources, or if the delivery schedule is neither pressing nor inflexible, the buyer is in a stronger bargaining position. Of course, neither side should let the other know explicitly how much it needs the other, even though both sides may have developed good ideas of this need during the period of negotiation.

At this stage of the game, success goes to the person with the best bargaining position or the courage to outwait the other. Outwaiting is sometimes difficult, especially if the seller wants the contract badly and is not sure how much competition is present in the procurement. But failure to say "No" and to go home to wait is sometimes the difference between a successful negotiation and a poor one. For example, a subcontractor was sent a purchase order for an item that he had been supplying to a particular firm for a number of years. The purchase order provided for redetermination. The seller had been selling the item on a fixed-price basis. The item represented one-third of his production and had a substantial profit margin, one far above that which the buyer would allow him in the event of redetermination. He analyzed his position in the following way. The item was complex and, to the best of his knowledge, he was the sole source. The item required a large investment in special tooling and facilities and considerable proprietary information for its manufacture. After considering these points, he told the buyer that he was unwilling to sell the item on other than a fixed-price basis. He heard nothing more from the buyer until the day before the expiration date on his original proposal, when he received a telegram conceding to his demand for a fixed-price contract. If he had lost his nerve, he would have sacrificed many thousands of dollars in profit over ensuing years. But note that many sellers have held out too long and lost substantial contracts.

When negotiations have broken down, it is sometimes difficult to get them started again. Each side should continue to develop its arguments, and if new ones are found, they should be presented. Each side should be on the alert to provide the other party with a face-saving out when the negotiation resumes. During this period, the seller must keep close watch to insure that the buyer is not, in fact, negotiating with an alternative source. Which side gives in first and accepts the other's offer depends on the circumstances of the procurement and the skill and courage of the negotiators involved.

Many buyers and sellers consider the negotiation finished when the price and the delivery schedule have been decided. It is just as important to reach agreement on all the technical points, delivery, terms, and price that make up the contract package.

Contracts and subcontracts are complex instruments with many detailed terms. Usually these terms affect both the seller's costs and the benefits he receives for performing the contract. For this reason, the seller must evaluate carefully all contractual terms in relation to cost and price to guarantee that the price he receives will compensate him for all of his efforts under the contract. Inspection, security, delivery, patent and technical data requirements, and many others have specific cost aspects.

It is important that a complete understanding be reached on all contractual terms during the negotiation. Many buyers feel that the seller understands the use of standard clauses and their effect on the contract, and will include them in the final contract. This feeling often makes it necessary to reopen negotiations in order to reach agreement on disputed points, and to prepare a correct contractual document. Substantial delays are incurred and much additional effort is expended in correcting a contract document. This can be prevented by spending additional time to check the list of clauses included to make sure that they properly belong in the contract and that each party understands specifically the application and meaning of each clause included. Particular attention should be given to non-standard clauses used by the different services. Sellers should carefully review contract terms, because in many cases, a minor change in wording can change substantially the meaning of a standard buyer clause regarding the rights and responsibilities of the seller.

As the majority of sellers expect to do business with their customers for a considerable period of time in the future, the seller must consider his future relations with the buyer as well as the immediate transaction. Submitting low initial quotations, performing contracts on schedule, and providing cooperation to the various technical, contracting, and inspection personnel of the buyer materially assists in developing a reputation of being a firm with whom people like to do business. A cooperative attitude during negotiation and the development of a good relationship also provide solid groundwork for securing favorable decisions on contested matters during the performance of the contract. In many cases, later contract administration problems may be more important and concern larger sums than the points at issue during the initial negotiation of the contract.

Both sides should make certain that a common understanding on the meaning of all contract clauses has been reached before terminating the final negotiation conference. If some vital conditions have been overlooked or misunderstood, the seller may find himself in the position of being forced to refuse to sign a contract when it is presented to him, making it necessary to reopen negotiations. Delays in starting work under the contract may ensue, with subsequent failure to meet delivery schedules, and, in some cases, with other costs to the seller if his production schedules are disrupted.

Therefore, it is desirable to put the essential terms of the agreement in writing before the negotiation conference ends. If the buyer seems unwilling to dictate the agreement himself, the seller should do so in his presence, particularly if there has been considerable difficulty in reaching agreement. Many buyers assume that sellers are completely familiar with the boiler-plate-type clauses used in their contracts. These clauses can have a substantial effect on the contract price and the services required from the seller.

The memorandum of understanding regarding negotiation should reference each clause in the final contract document. This is important, because in many cases the personnel negotiating the contract do not draft the final contract. The document may be drafted by the legal department, which will use, unless otherwise instructed, standard contract clauses that, in many cases, are not applicable to the type of contract under consideration. An additional short period of time spent in going over the list of clauses to be included in the contract will save considerable renegotiation time. The contract written as a result of the negotiation will represent accurately the intent of the parties.

Under certain circumstances, buyers and sellers must submit actually or by specific identification in writing cost or pricing data and certify that to the best of their knowledge and belief, the cost and pricing data submitted is accurate, complete, and current.

Cost or pricing data can be defined as all the facts existing up to the time of agreement on price which prudent buyers and sellers would reasonably expect to have a significant effect on the price negotiation. If defective data is furnished, the buyer is entitled to an adjustment of the negotiated price, including profit or fee, to exclude any significant sum by which the price was increased because of the defective data.

Often during negotiation it becomes apparent that certain data may be considered defective within the meaning of the regulation. The validity of this data is considered by the buyer and seller in the agreed-upon total price that compromises all the issues in the negotiation. It is extremely important that this data be identified and its effect on the final settlement be carefully documented in the final negotiation memorandum. If this is not done, the seller may find that even though both he and the buyer considered the defective data in their final deal, he is still subject to a request for a refund. Many contracts have clauses which provide that in the absence of evidence to the contrary, the natural and probable consequence of defective data is an increase in the contract price in the amount of the defect plus related burden and profit or fee; therefore, unless there is a clear indication that the defective data was not used, or was not relied upon, the contract price should be reduced in that amount.

Index

147

About the Author

Neal W. Beckmann, C.P.M., is general manager, BBC National Procurement, a division of Bank Building and Equipment Corporation of America. He is a member of the board of directors, Purchasing Management Association of St. Louis (P.M.A.S.L.), a member of the National Association of Purchasing Management (N.A.P.M.), International Federation of Purchasing and Materials Management (I.F.P.M.M.), and vice-chairman of the Minority Purchasing Council of Metropolitan St. Louis. He has served as alderman, park commissioner, director-youth activities, director-senior citizens activities, and member of the Cub Scout Executive Board in Edmundson, Missouri. He is the recipient of the Khoury League Sportsman Award for Community Service. Mr. Beckmann is a visiting lecturer at Washington University and St. Louis University, and a frequent speaker at lectures and seminars throughout the nation. He has written extensively on negotiations and purchasing including such articles as "The Right Personnel for Negotiations," "Negotiations Are Not Just For Lowering the Purchase Price," and "Purchasing's Role In The Make-Or-Buy Decision." He served in the U.S. Army (Aviation) during the Vietnam conflict and is currently pursuing associate degrees in materials management and management sciences. Mr. Beckmann has served as negotiating and purchasing consultant to many industrial firms and received designation as Certified Purchasing Manager in November, 1975.